How to Become a Woman of *Charme*
The Ultimate Guide to Timeless Style

(Black and white edition)

HOW TO BE GLAMOROUS, STYLISH, AND CHIC AND
ACHIEVE A SOPHISTICATED LOOK AND UNIQUE FRENCH
ALLURE THROUGH NO-COST IDEAS AND FASHION
ADVICE THAT ENHANCE BEAUTY AND SELF-CONFIDENCE
FOR WOMEN OF ANY BODY SHAPE

Chiara Giuliani

TRANSLATED BY
VICTORIA AND CONNOR DE MALEY

Illustrations by
Isaxar-Filitova-Zzveillust
/shutterstock.com

© 2017 Chiara Giuliani
All rights reserved.

Illustrations:
© 2017 Isaxar/Shutterstock.com
© 2017 Filitova/Shutterstock.com
© 2017 Zzveillust/Shutterstock.com

Cover illustrations:
© 2017 Isaxar/Shutterstock.com
© 2017 artsandra/Shutterstock.com

All rights reserved.

ISBN-13: 978-1974325986
ISBN-10: 1974325989

Website:
www.ladonnadicharme.it

To my mother

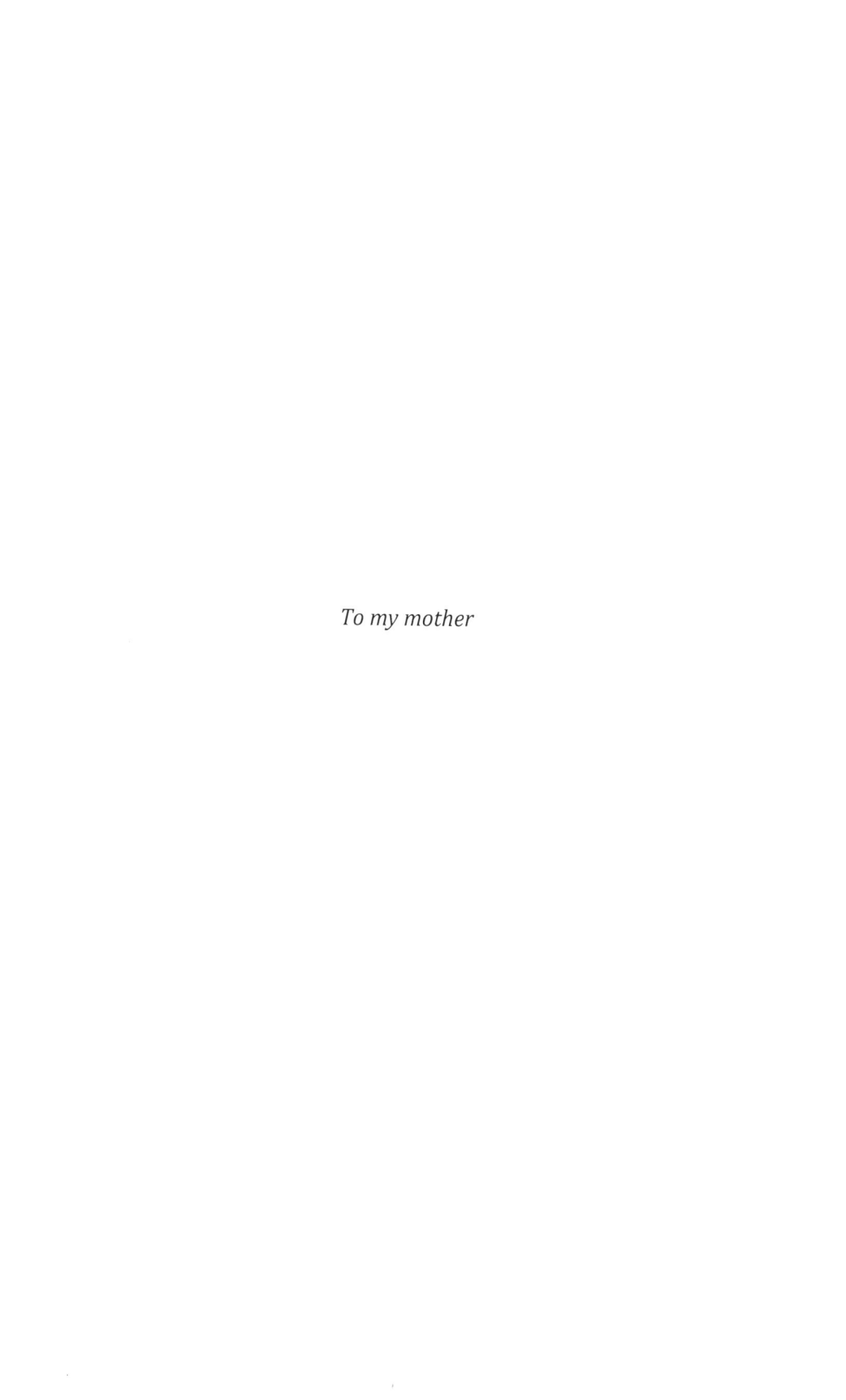

ACKNOWLEDGMENTS

*I'd like to thank from the bottom of my heart
all my friends from near and far, who are the true
and irreplaceable sources of inspiration for this book.*

Contents

Preface: The Meaning of Charme 7
Introduction: Style and Fashion 11

PART ONE: FINDING YOUR OWN STYLE

I. The Secret to Style: Rediscovering Femininity 17
II. The Informal Woman: Between Simplicity and Whimsy 20
III. The Classic Woman: Stability and Tradition 26
IV. The Sophisticated Woman: Grace and Flawlessness 32
V. The Sexy Woman: Breezy Sensuality 38
VI. The Sporty Woman: Classy Informality 44
VII. The Green Woman: Natural Simplicity 50
VIII. The Trendy Woman: Fashion Tailor-Made 56
IX. The Artistic Woman: Creative and Unconventional 62
X. Extremes to Avoid: Fashion Victim,
  Overbranded, and Alternative to the Bitter End 68

PART TWO: THE PRACTICAL RULES OF *CHARME*

XI. Rules and Personality 77
XII. Colors: The Nuances of Charme 80
XIII. Patterns and Shapes: The Secret of Proportion 89
  To seem a bit taller 91
  To seem a bit thinner 93
  For those who'd like to have more curves 97

XIV. Fabric and Materials: The Importance of Yarn from Linen to Wool	100
XV. The Secrets to Versatility: Accessories	106
XVI. What Should I Wear Today? Character and Personality for Every Occasion	114
XVII. Let's Party! Charming Outfits for Special Occasions	123
XVIII. The Closet: How to Organize It Perfectly in Three Steps	131

PART THREE: TIMELESS *CHARME*

XIX. Charme and Style at Any Age	139
XX. Retro *Charme*: Learning from the Past	146
XXI. Timeless Style: The Appeal of Personality	157
XXII. Wrapping It All Up in Beauty: The 7 Rules of Style (And Some Clichés to Demystify)	162

APPENDIX - FABRICS AND TEXTILES: THE WEAVE OF STYLE

Preface

The Meaning of *Charme*

Of course, you're pretty short. The strange thing is that people never notice it. You only notice it when someone is standing near you.

This observation was made to me by a friend when I was a teenager (naturally, at thirteen years old, no one can be expected to be a champion of diplomacy). Those words, said with ingenuity, actually didn't bother me much; instead, they were useful to make me aware, beyond any doubt, of the fact that I *really* was quite small. (Today we would use the term *petite,* but in those days the word was *short,* and that was about it.)

What's more interesting, though, is the second part of the phrase, that "people never notice it," which, when looked at closely, reveals one of the secrets of feminine *charme*, a **French word** whose meaning is slightly different from the English word *charm* and indicates "**an ensemble of beauty, elegance, appeal, allure, and style.**"

As a matter of fact, the **beauty and allure of a woman** are so much more than just long legs, deep eyes, and luscious hair; beauty is brought about by the **holistic effect of many elements, including personality**, which can make a woman extremely attractive.

So **if we want to get a breathtaking look**, if we want people to remember us as charming, chic, and attractive, the first thing we have to do is really **plumb the depths of our personality**, and in this book we're going to see just how to do that.

We'll explain why **it just isn't enough to buy the patterns most suitable to our physiques** or the colors that match with the colors of our face **if we don't bother to make the most of our personality as well**.

We've all had one of those situations where we just weren't able to pull off the desired look, even when paying meticulous attention to all the color and pattern suggestions from the magazines and blogs.

And do you know why that happens? Because the secret of femininity—and thus **the secret of** *charme*—comes from the **harmony of our face, our physique, *and our personality***, all of which is **enhanced by the femininity that each one of us possesses**.

And so the basic guidelines for matching between a certain body type and the most appropriate patterns/colors/outfits aren't sufficient on their own to guarantee a satisfying result—not if the choices we make aren't aligned with our personality.

Because even the most beautiful, well-crafted, and classy piece of clothing ends up looking disastrous if put on a woman without reflecting her style.

Meanwhile, even **the simplest of jeans can produce stupendous results as long as they're in character with the femininity of the woman wearing them**.

In the pages to come, we're going to first **see how to identify the style that works best for us**, the one that's most in keeping with our personality and allows us to feel at ease no matter where we are.

When we're picking out our outfits, we cannot only consider those things that vibe with our physique and bring out its best qualities; we must also be sure to also **choose those items that**

match up with our deep nature, making it shine and allowing us to feel like ourselves just like, if not more than, how a dress with a perfect cut would. When we choose our clothing more wisely, we'll be able zero in with maximum clarity on whatever it is that makes us feel true to ourselves, **more self-confident**, and, as a result, **much more beautiful and captivating**.

Then we'll go on to look at how it's possible to **camouflage the majority of our so-called imperfections**, sometimes even turning them into strengths, **with a shrewd management of clothing, accessories, and colors**, but also by increasing the appeal of our personality, which is the secret of that *charme* that every woman wishes she had.

We're also going to analyze the various **components of an outfit, including colors, models, fabrics**, and also address the many different daily occasions that dictate which clothes are worn—this will provide us tools with which we can personalize our style and express ourselves in a million and one ways.

When all's said and done, remember that a face that isn't exactly regular but is rather more interesting, that reflects a determined personality and is enriched by **an outfit in tone with the character of whoever's wearing it** turns out to look **so much more attractive** than a perfect face that's easily forgotten.

We'll also see that **beauty and appeal have nothing to do with the shape of our body**. A fuller-figured woman, accompanied by a character and clothing that play to her strengths, can walk away from the closet looking just as if not more attractive and put together than an excessively thin woman (in spite of the perennial diets to which we subject ourselves).

In this book, alongside many technical suggestions, we'll find the encouragement to **look inside ourselves** to find our style, the one that helps us feel irresistibly beautiful, forever at ease, and uniquely ourselves.

For a woman, being beautiful—or even better, to jump a step above simple beauty, **feeling alluring and irresistible—can actually be incredibly easy**.

That's because a woman, meaning **a woman of all physiques, *always* has the possibility of becoming beautiful *if she listens to her own sty*le**.

Always remember that, just as the unforgettable Coco Chanel said, "Beauty begins the moment you decide to be yourself."

And so, if you're browsing the pages of this volume, this means that you're already almost there, because **deciding to become attractive and feel beautiful while remaining always yourself is the first step to truly reaching it**.

Introduction

Style and Fashion

> *Fashion is made to become unfashionable.*
> —Coco Chanel

The yearning to understand how our clothes can enhance our physique has always been a necessity for me: less than five-foot-two and having grown up around a bunch of incredibly tall friends (my best friend from high school was a model!), I learned by **experimenting on my own** to see how **combinations of color, patterns, and accessories** most in line with who I was could **transform my figure** while also helping my personality shine.

When I was a teenager in the '80s, fashion wasn't like it is now. There were very few techniques to making yourself attractive at that time: high heels were practically nonexistent, only worn by grandmothers and aunts; shoes were almost religiously black; and the clothes of any and every type were formless, failing to offer even minimum support to those who, like me, perhaps would have liked to seem a little bit thinner and more feminine.

The only solution I had was going DIY: modeling clothes on myself and studying the fabrics and color tones.

By doing this over the years, I was able to **learn the tricks of the trade when it came to putting a spotlight on our best features** in a way that could be timeless with respect to the changeability of the trends.

I have to admit, though, that in the beginning the things I came up with weren't all that satisfying: the clothes that I was picking out made my physique stand out, but they often weren't right for certain occasions, nor did they mesh a whole lot with my way of being.

Sure, I was more good-looking, but I did not have any *charme* yet.

It took some time for me to understand that **in order to succeed, every stylistic choice must come from our nature**, and so it's fundamental that we understand ourselves for who we are in order to milk everything out of our potential.

Only in this way can we truly understand just what is the *right* choice for each one of us, discovering the path we must follow so that we can come up with **uniquely alluring outfits that fully reflect our personality and our spirit**.

These days, among other things, there is such a vast selection of clothing options that **every one of us has the possibility of finding items that bring out the best** in us.

Despite this, however, so many of us find ourselves confronting the daily dilemma of "What am I going to wear today?", and all too often our choices leave us underwhelmed or at least partially so.

I often see young women in the street wearing clothes that are perfectly formed for their physique, each one of them wearing up-to-the-minute fashion, and yet they are anything but alluring or beautiful.

The reason for these failures lies essentially in the fact that **when we follow the trends,** we very often find ourselves **forgetting the importance of sticking to our own style**, which is fundamental if we want to craft an image that not only keeps us satisfied but also profoundly reflects us, **highlighting our physique as well as our character**.

Only **style**, in the end, is able to **fully bring out our best**.

As Coco Chanel said, "Fashion changes, but style endures". **And so it's style, not fashion, that we have to follow.**

This book, then, through suggestions, tips, and practical examples, seeks to be a kind of practical guide to rediscover ourselves (from an aesthetic point of view, but not only), pointing out useful recommendations for playing up and **highlighting our strong points and mitigating our imperfections**, making use also of **ideas offered from time to time by fashion but without being slavish about it**.

It's important to remember that the patterns proposed by current fashion trends don't take into account any of the inevitable differences, be they physical or personality-based, that distinguish each one of us. So **we can of course make use of fashion**, as discussed above, **but always in *our* own way**, because fashion is undeniably funny and striking, but following it too religiously can actually lead us further away from the thing we all want in the first place: style.

In this guide, we'll be looking at **the principal styles that correspond to the many different facets of personality**, which necessarily constitute **the first and fundamental point of departure**, because clearly identifying what style is for each one of us, what suits us best according to our personality, is the first step toward being able to feel our best no matter the context.

In this book, you'll learn some guidelines that will help you find the most suitable style for you and will help you become the lodestar to follow in order to **obtain that timeless *charme* that all women across all ages can have**.

From the careful attention to **detail, soft colors, and harmonious forms**, to the **rediscovery of fine fabrics** in which the weave and the yarn recount their story and the color declares its accents, *this* is the *charme* we're looking for. Born from smiles and attention, from kindness and harmony in how we get along with others and carry ourselves (even if by chance...even if for just one minute), this *charme* is carried out with the sensibility and perceptiveness that has always distinguished women in society.

From there you'll encounter **practical advice and style reflections**, but you'll also get suggestions on how to be an **attentive shopper** and how to seem as though you've just walked out of a boutique shop even if the majority of your outfit came at a cost of no more than twenty-five dollars.

I hope that the pointers and advice in this book prove useful in improving your relationship with the daily moment of picking out your everyday outfit and also, at least a little bit, your relationship with yourself as well as with those around you.

Always remember that **every last one of us is unique**, and it's only through understanding ourselves and bringing out our best qualities that we can make the most of who we are.

Enjoy the read!

PART ONE

Finding Your Own Style

I. The Secret to Style: Rediscovering Femininity

Style is having courage in our choices, but also the courage to say no.
—*Giorgio Armani*

Finding your own style is, at the end of the day, really quite simple. There's just one key: truly **embracing your own sense of femininity**.

In truth, there are many ways to be a woman, and each one of these perfectly corresponds to a well-defined style born from the fusion of our aesthetic taste and our own personality.

It's precisely because of this that we can say that it's enough to simply **reach into our own way of being a woman** and our character **to find the style that brings out the most in us**—the one that fits us the best.

But what does that even mean?

It means, in other words, that if we consciously gear our aesthetic choices toward styles that reflect who we are, with just a teensy bit of effort we will be able to achieve **our most personalized style**, which will have a double advantage. On the one hand, it will help us make the most out of ourselves aesthetically, and on the other hand, it will help us understand ourselves even better, something that can only happen if our style is in synch with our nature.

In selecting our look—for example, when we pick out our daily outfit—**personality is of far more importance than the**

use of aesthetic ideals, which may be formally irreproachable but are not personalized in any way.

I'm sure you've seen a friend for whom look is usually not of huge importance all dressed up for an important occasion and looking no more attractive than usual and even looking clumsy and impeded by clothes in which she clearly feels uncomfortable. This is the most evident proof of how important it is to always follow your own personal style, one that descends from your own inner nature and personality, **pairing this rule with some necessary technical suggestions to enhance your physical characteristics**.

In and of itself, as you can see, the concept is pretty simple.

What's a bit less simple is translating it into something that can be readily put into use.

To better understand what this means, let's try to shed some light on it with a comparison of the color of a simple piece of clothing. Take an everlasting color: blue, for example. Without a doubt, this is a classic color that goes well with practically anything, one that everyone tends to like. Each one of us, however, will use the color blue in a slightly different way.

This is because each one of us will chose a different tonality of blue, even if that hue varies only just slightly, and also because despite using the same color, we will always choose combinations that will make it seem different.

A woman with a more exuberant character will tend to prefer, for instance, more brightly lit tonalities, almost electric blue. The traditionalist wills her preference to the classic navy blue. A woman with a more romantic nature will match her blue with pink floral patterns, and so it goes.

This selection process usually gets carried out in a completely spontaneous and unconscious way, at least for the simplest of choices, such as color or pattern. But if we apply it to our whole personal look in a deliberately conscious way, our decisions will have the effect of clearly **highlighting what fits and matches us the best** and what brings out the best in us.

If we **focus on the most significant aspects of our personality** and our character and **combine them with the choices that bring out the magic of our body type**, we will then be able to zero in on the most suitable look for us, avoiding having closets stuffed to the brim with clothes that we will never even think about putting on. The end result? Allowing us to have **a curated choice rather than an unlimited one**.

A closet overflowing with clothes and accessories, rather than giving us the opportunity to have the most perfect outfit for every occasion, instead **drains us of our energy** as we waste time choosing and mixing up our ideas; it can leave us feeling indecisive.

In contrast, having but just **the right amount of clothing for us** allows us to always roll on the safe side of things and **feel "right" in every occasion**.

In the next pages, we will cover the main styles. We are going to see how we can trace their origins, which are founded on our character type and on our personality. The idea came to me while I was observing my dearest friends; I realized how for each certain type of character, there was a corresponding well-defined understanding of image and self-care.

As I mentioned in the beginning, the styles are not picked out like the typically understood aesthetic standards, but instead they should be seen as the many facets of the diverse ways of expressing your own femininity. For this reason in particular, **they transcend the trends of the day and the passage of time**.

This allows us to be, in every moment and in all occasions, **authentically fascinating and spontaneously feminine**.

Because it's truly our femininity—and let's not forget it—that at once contains and reveals the *charme* of every woman.

How to Become a Woman of Charme

II. The Informal Woman: Between Simplicity and Whimsy

Here's Bianca, an outgoing and spontaneous woman. Dependable and kind, she gives off the impression of always being at ease in her own skin, an **every-moment and all-occasions kind of woman**.

She has a way of being pleasantly feminine that makes everyone around her feel like the center of her attention, but at the same time she possesses the tendency to mediate everything around her and lessen the stress of a situation so that it's manageable, encouraging others to do likewise.

She doesn't waste her time with conventions.

A very formal evening dress, for her, would be a little bit over the top. And yet she always manages to seem absolutely put-together and at ease. **Even in the most formal situations, she nails it, but, incredibly, with an outfit that is indisputably informal.**

What's her secret?

Well, first of all, she's endowed with the capacity to combine in a unique way clothes that are so simple that if worn by another woman they could appear anonymous, adding only **a slightly impalpable touch that makes her personality pop out.**

This allows her to feel beautiful and attractive no matter the context, transmitting this sensation to those around her, with the result that everybody finds her *very* attractive.

In addition to all this, over the years Bianca has **defined and consolidated just what exactly is best for her**, both in terms of colors and prints and fabrics, with the final result being that each combination she wears is a smash success while at the same time seeming marvelously spur-of-the-moment.

After all, her **spontaneity** is another one of her features that sets her apart. And thanks to this, despite always seeming breezily flawless, that little touch of coldness that sometimes you can get a sense of behind an overthought outfit is eliminated.

Now let's take a close look at what distinguishes Bianca's style, which is what I would define as an "informal style" (and which many others might call casual despite that fact that, in reality, her style is not casual at all).

The characteristics of this style aren't easy to pinpoint, since—as the name makes abundantly clear—the main characteristic is informality, by which we mean the absence of true and proper formal and stylistic references.

Specifically for this reason, it's **one of the most authentic and versatile styles around**, easily adaptable for all seasons and specifications.

With that said, it's no wonder that this is one of the most loved and most widespread styles of women of all ages.

What makes this style jump out more than anything else is primarily the presence of **basic elements that we could define as impervious to the passage of time and trends** (without really being "classics" in the strictest sense) and which adapt and mold themselves to the characteristics of the women wearing them, bringing out their best again and again while tossing aside any imperfections.

Let's start, for example, with the clothes samples and patterns. They're **never too traditional, nor should they be excessively avant-garde**. They're usually versatile clothes with simple cuts that are not too tight. Cigarette pants, smartly tailored shirts, and knee-length skirts are all perfect examples, generally of a size chosen so that the form adapts magically and easily to the physical form of those wearing them, and this can even be enhanced by the addition of an accessory—even a small one—

that personalizes the whole package, making what you're wearing unique and recognizable. (In part 2 of the book, we will cover all the "technical" suggestions for choosing the most appropriately sized clothing for each physical type.)

Even the colors of these informal outfits contain multitudes of possibilities, ranging from the untouchable black and white all the way to blue and then even on to denim, matched with **some bright colors** or some stroke of imagination to make them pop.

A pair of jeans with a jacket with special finishes make the Informal Woman's outfit perfect: practical, but fit for all occasions.

The tendency is to combine them all together in a highly personal way, avoiding the tone-on-tone approach (a more frequent take, as we'll see later, in other styles) but in a no less harmonious or pleasing stylization.

The use of color is given a new life—or accentuated—by bouncing off colors selected from those that lend themselves to her overall complexion: even here, just this little bit of a touch of personalization can **give an expertly curated aspect to even the simplest of outfits**.

Accessories, as opposed to basic garments, are generally inventive and uniquely personalized, even if their choice process is always thoughtful, to avoid overloading the whole outfit.

This style, in fact, leaves much **open to the imagination when thinking of how to accessorize**, thanks to the fact that, with respect to other styles, the selection in this case can be much vaster, because the sobriety and the simplicity of the overall outfit gives us the liberty to experiment a bit more liberally with accessories, gifting us almost free rein to do whatever we want while guaranteeing that it is absolutely in character.

Now, as for hair and makeup, what makes the Informal Woman shine the most is a **natural but crafted effect**, something that refuses to totally reshape the natural characteristics of each individual while also adding a hint of fun and surprise.

As far as hair goes, it should always be taken care of in a way that really makes your natural hair color burst: a woman who has brown hair should be able to go for a slightly more luminous shade of brown, while a blond woman would be able to opt for a few more soft highlights to make it work.

For sure, we can't be having any sudden and unsettling twists from blond to jet black or vice versa.

And yet, sometimes, even while remaining true to her natural color, the Informal Woman often enjoys experimenting with different hairstyles, moving effortlessly from a smooth bob to a wonderfully curly and disheveled look.

As always, it just depends on your mood in a given season.

Makeup should have the most natural effect possible: slight foundation; little or no blush; delicate mascara, selected according to the color of the eyebrow; and very little lipstick (typically, the Informal Woman goes for lip gloss instead).

In the way of a surprise, then, **an accessory, small but tasteful**, placed in the hair can go a long way. Or if not that, then a streak of an unusual eye shadow that really brings out the depth of the eyes can be striking.

All of this for **a magnetic look** that draws all attention to an outfit that, upon closer inspection, you can't really figure out what makes it shine so emphatically.

Oh, but what a particular shine it is.

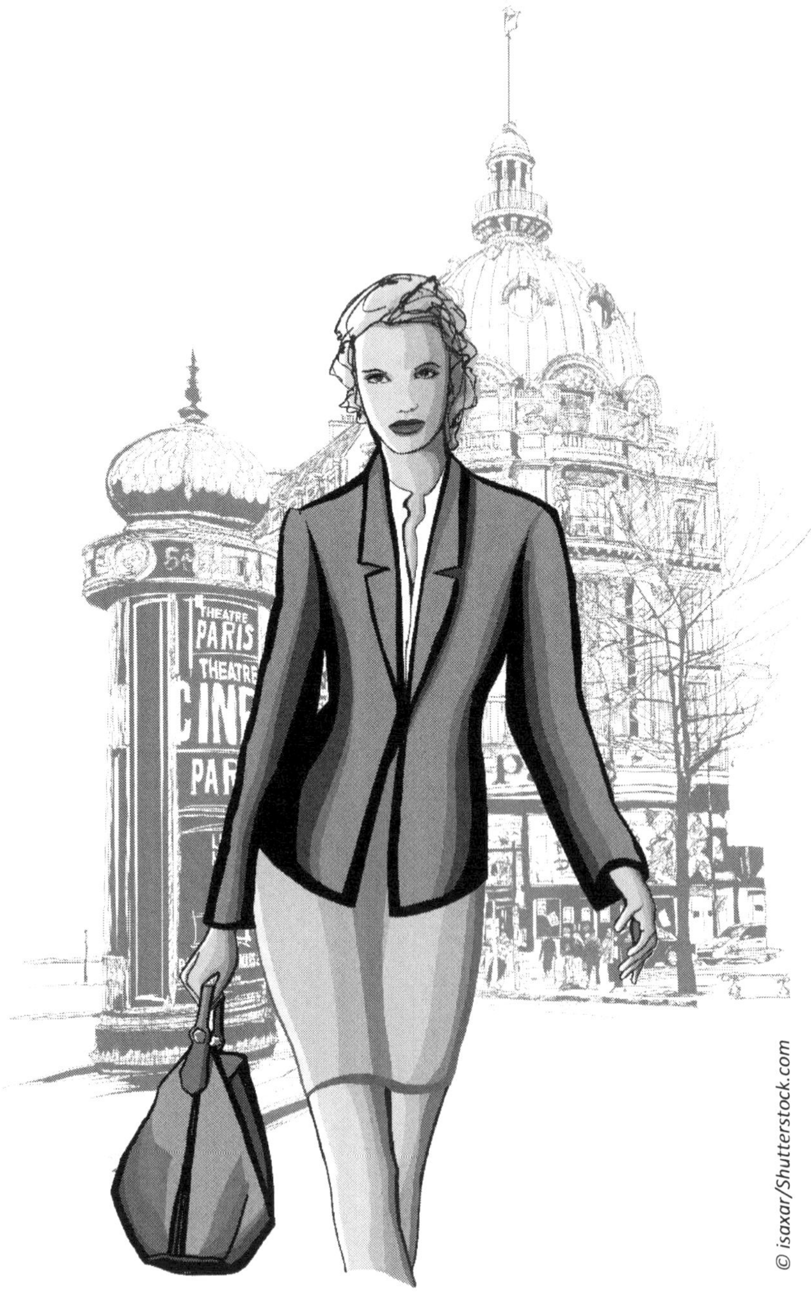
THEATRE
PARIS
THEATRE
PAR

III. The Classic Woman: Stability and Tradition

Here we have Angela, the paragon of a Classic Woman. With a **reserved but steadfast personality**, she doesn't really love being the center of attention or highlighting herself too much.

Despite this, she's always able to capture the focus of those who are around her thanks to her characteristic way of being **delightfully low-key**, equally as discrete as she is, on the flipside, appreciated by those in her company.

She spontaneously **eludes trends of any and all varieties**, sometimes unconsciously and other times by choice.

You'll never, ever catch her in a pair of skin-tight ripped jeans that are bleach-faded perfectly on purpose, not even at fifteen years old.

Carelessness in one's choices of clothes—as well as in one's behavior—**strikes her almost as an offense**. Just to prove it, if you asked her, she would tell you that always being put together is, for her, a form of respect for others in addition to being a pleasure in its own right.

Her style, far from being unassuming or outdated, is a sweetly traditional kind of fashion that is purely in step at all times with her character and her sense of self.

And yet, despite her desire to not make herself noticed, it's a style that also never allows Angela to remain unnoticed either, neither in the circles of her closest friends nor in places where her familiarity of the people is more superficial—and this, despite any reticence, is what makes her stand apart from the rest.

Another one of her strengths, found both in her character and her clothing, is **consistency**, something Angela turns into an issue of principal.

Her way in the world is delightfully predictable, which makes her into a **reassuring point of reference**, a support system you can always count on.

One of her best qualities is her unflinching reliability. If you have her at your side, you can rest assured that you have a constant connection, quiet but strong and tenacious.

Her way of understanding fashion is consistently the exact mirror of her character. (I mean, how could it be otherwise?) She'll never be caught dead in a showy, gaudy piece of clothing or something else that could draw too much attention to her. But nevertheless, **she always manages to have, undeniably, nothing but class**.

There is a wonderful phrase of Christian Dior's that seems to have been written solely for Angela: "True elegance is wearing what goes unnoticed in the underground."

Thanks to her inborn sense of style, Angela knows how to match everything from garments to patterns to colors, and she also has the ability to **single out with total confidence the most suitable garment for each occasion**—this is, after all, the secret of true elegance—and pulling off, without fail, a **look that remains absolutely form-fitting to context, always polished and always elegant**.

So what, then, distinguishes a "classic" style anyway?

Before anything else, it's concretely based on a series of garments that are impervious to time, done with **fabrics and textiles of high quality and craftsmanship**, whose quality is maintained throughout the years.

The patterns are traditional, usually smooth, and never too tight to the body.

Even when the reigning fashion trends of the day call for miniskirts and stretch pants, the Classic Woman gives her preference to skirts and tailored pants with **simple and linear cuts, not too flashy or ostentatious**, which adapt themselves softly to her body. At most, should the desire for a slightly different look come up, she might decide to shorten the hem of the skirt by just a few centimeters—from four to two centimeters below the knee—but absolutely no more than that.

Seldom are you likely to find T-shirts in her closet. Dress shirts, however, abound in her wardrobe, always muted and simple but sometimes tempered by **some charming details**.

Particularly suitable are **twinsets**, a truly failsafe garment ready to add class to even the simplest of outfits.

Long-sleeve knit sweaters can be both cardigan-style or V-neck (combined with shirts, both the most classic and feminine style) or even turtlenecks, perhaps accompanied by a string of pearls or a classic necklace. **The use of imaginative junk jewelry isn't even remotely considered.**

For formal occasions, she often goes for classic pantsuits made with high-quality fabrics and only the best craftsmanship, alternating the classic jacket and skirt to the pantsuits that are normally only reserved for the workplace because, although elegant, they're all too often considered insufficiently feminine.

Synthetic fabrics, wild prints, and garments of a gaudy color or pattern are obviously banished from her closet, equally as much for clothing as for accessories.

And since we're on the topic of colors, aside from the classic blacks, blues, grays, browns, beiges, and whites, her preferred hues are, surprisingly, also dark reds and dark purples for winter, and pastel colors for the summer season, with which every now and then she plays around a bit by bringing a breath of fun and imagination to her usually consistent choices in clothing. Red, worn by Angela, becomes the most classic color of all.

The use of **accessories** in a style like this is moderate, almost **reduced to a bare minimum**. It goes without saying that the choice comes down to **only high-quality articles that remain timeless**.

Bags should be strictly made of leather and usually of a dark color, excepting some gray bags that are allowed in the summer months. They should be amply sized without being *too* big: usually, the Classic Woman has some rather serious-minded habits and stays away from stuffing her bags full of the kinds of stuff (makeup, hairbrushes, magazines, books, curlers, or boxes of diet bars) that is fairly typical for many women.

For shoes, the same holds true: high-quality leather with exclusively dark colors in the wintertime, and lighter shades in the summer, with heels that one would define as *reasonable*—not devoid of height completely but not overly high or really slender either.

And, contrary to how much it happens to the vast majority of women, the Classic Woman usually **doesn't have an unmanageable number of shoes and bags**. Three or four well-made pairs each are decisively more than sufficient for her to last a whole season.

As for all the other accessories, the Classic Woman's usage of these is practically zero with the exception of some belts here or there, whose color is usually chosen to match the pants or, sometimes, the shoes. The only exception, as we've seen, would be the classic string of pearls or a similar kind of necklace, maybe made with bone, to round off the look and give her that final dash of class that adapts itself to every environment and all occasions.

Hair care, on the other hand, isn't merely a meticulous fuss, but rather a **clearly visible aspect**. Hairstyling is an absolutely indispensable moment for her because, as she knows, when it comes to the image of a woman, hair cannot go ignored. It goes without saying that **the preferred cut is modest, neither too long nor too short**. In general, she prefers something like a medium length, ending just slightly under the ear or, at most, the neck, leaving the face uncovered and without clumps or fringes of any kind. Over time, it will vary slightly, and the color may vary slightly as well. This last bit here is maybe the only observation you can make to the Classic Woman: the face changes over time, no doubt, and so even the color and the cut may have to be gently modified so that they conform to the face and soften the features.

On the subject of **makeup**, the following is eternally true: the Classic Woman would consider leaving the house without having made herself up to be a sign of carelessness and a lack of femininity. What it comes down to are the tones: absolutely **neutral, discreet, and almost imperceptible**—giving the face a nice, neat look without shouting for attention.

This last detail, together with an outfit that might sometimes come off as a bit too precise, by contrast makes the face appear young and fresh, with a **light and pleasant overall effect, classy beyond a shadow of a doubt**.

How to Become a Woman of Charme

IV. The Sophisticated Woman: Grace and Flawlessness

Rebecca is a decisive and determined kind of woman, softened by **impeccable manners** and an innate kindness of spirit, hidden behind an attitude that at first glance seems distracted but in reality masks a **genuine concern for others**.

Always attentive to form, she also appreciates the company of spontaneous and imaginative people, as long as that spontaneity doesn't go beyond the bounds of the occasion.

Polite and discreet, she's the ideal confidant for any eventuality, because you can always count on her to never, not even under torture, reveal what you've told her, nor will she ever judge you for it.

Her style can be characterized like this: she usually prefers clothes that are **classic in their own way without being too traditional** in the common sense of the term, and she matches them with items that on another person might seem showy but in her case pass almost unnoticed, emphasizing by contrast the extreme linearity and the classic traditionalism of the number she's wearing.

On her, even a pair of jeans can become classic and refined.

And a pair of super traditional medium-heeled loafers, worn nonchalantly in a period when loafers are considered totally outside the fashion world, hardly gives off an outdated vibe. No, on her, it's the opposite: she appears almost like an avant-garde nonconformist, as if she anticipated the trend rather than following it.

Thanks to her innate fine taste, she's able to identify **unusual combinations that, over time, become the new classic look**.

Her preferences lead her to choose clothes with patterned lines and well-finished cuts, made with soft fabrics, sometimes with a visible weave (especially in the winter).

Color-wise, she keeps things largely traditional: blues and whites before all others, along with cream, beige, bordeaux, gray, brown—selected, however, in unusual tones with the nuances always being in harmony and **with the addition, as soon as possible, of an accent color that enhances everything**.

The use of black is more toned down, usually worn when softened with a combination of light-colored details or with some luminously accented accessories.

Warm colors like yellow, red, and orange—typically not seen as classic colors—are often used as dashes of color to make her outfit unique in her own way, like red shoes with a midnight-blue sweater-pants combination, or a yellow bag paired with a totally black outfit.

Another way she uses warm colors is as "accent" colors, complementary to the prevalent shades of the outfit. For example, she might pair an orange bag with an outfit dominated by gray-blue.

Careful attention is paid, however, to any flights of whimsy, which are usually kept to a minimum (scarves or shoes, for example).

As for **patterns**, she generally prefers outfits with a **feminine but simple form**: the classic sheath dress is a perfect example of what she has in mind, chosen in unexpected colors and usually knee-length, which also happens to be the desired length for coats and winter jackets.

*The use of minimal but carefully selected accessories
is one of the major characteristics of the Fashionable Woman*

She keeps the use of **accessories** to a strategic minimum. As we've seen, sometimes these can be **used for unusual and attractive color effects**—in particular with shoes, bags, and scarves—but as for the rest of the time, they are kept to a strict minimum, given that **simplicity** is one of the most defining features of this look, right down to the **meticulous attention to detail**.

Jewelry and hair accessories are practically nonexistent. On the other hand, bags, scarves, and shoes, as well as gloves and hats, are always subject to a careful and well-considered selection process, giving preference to **high-quality items** with a truly classic cut, but one that's not too excessively traditional.

A timeless sheath dress paired with high-quality accessories provides a simple but classy outfit.

Usually, she prefers shoes and sandals with heels that are quite high but rarely stilettos. Boots are typically knee-high, sometimes with low heels, and should never be, to be clear, ankle boots.

The **colors of the shoes** vary from more traditional tones in all shades and nuances (from natural leather to gray all the way to dark brown) to **lighter tones, frequently used also in the winter months**.

During spring and summer, aside from light brown and beige, she'll add pastels (pink powder, yellow) and bright colors, evened out by the monochromatic tones of the rest of the outfit.

Both for bags as well as for shoes, the use of black is restrained to cases where it's almost imperative or in combination with white, or with other tones that weaken the rigorous effect of the black.

Restrained dimensions and fixed forms prevail as far as bags. The colors can be pretty light also in the winter months, with a preference for more neutral tones of natural leather or dove gray, light gray, and beige. A few concessions are possible, even in this case, for some brighter items.

Similar to the Classic Woman, **hair and makeup are part of the look but done without attracting too much attention**.

For the hair, she usually goes for a medium-long cut, frequently preferring a straight, long bob or occasionally gathering it all up into a nice bun.

She pays close attention to her makeup while keeping it moderate with an almost invisible effect at first glance, but it's always carefully done.

It's the perfect complement for a style that, despite being made exclusively with traditional clothes and a minimum of flashiness, has an **absolutely charming effect**, making her strong and decisive personality spread around her.

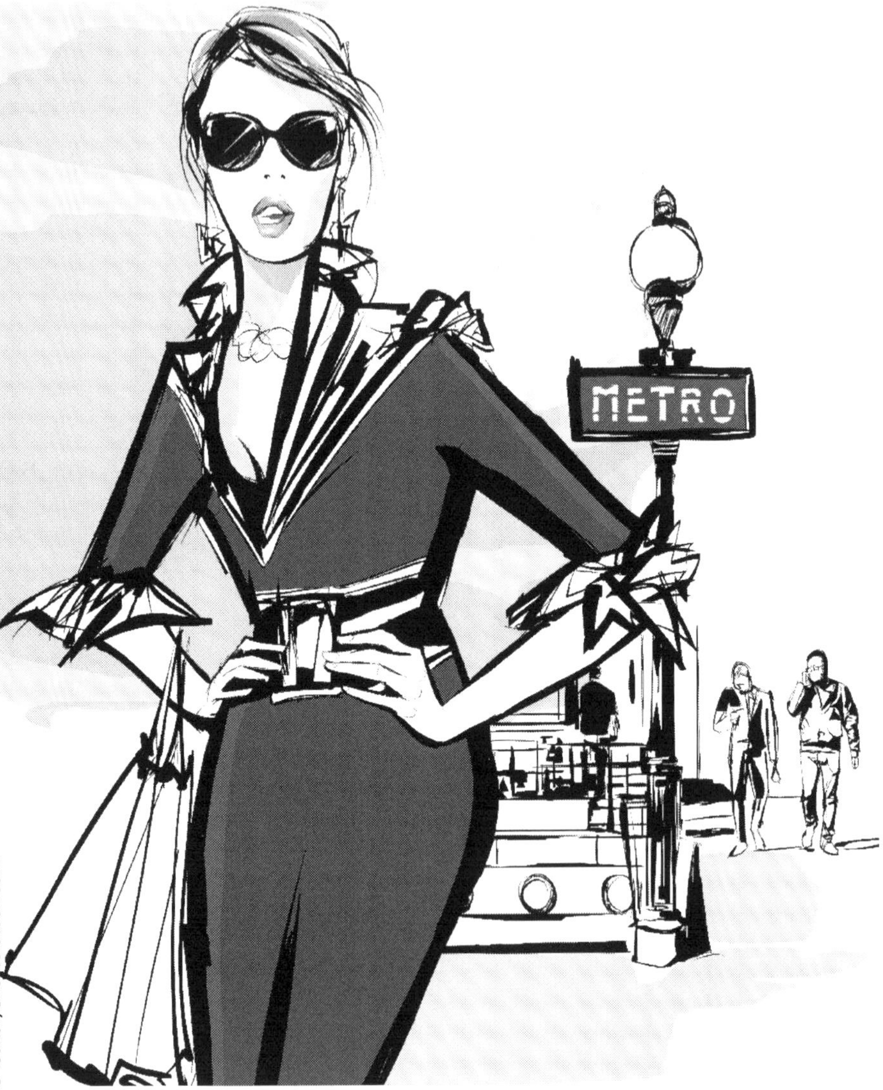
METRO

V. The Sexy Woman: Breezy Sensuality

Sofia is a **decidedly seductive** woman.

High heels and miniskirts, items that for other women are generally reserved for eveningwear or particular occasions, make up the basis of her daily outfit.

You'll never catch her out without makeup, unkempt, or with hair out of place. If she really, really has to wear a tracksuit, it'll probably be a fluorescent one, tight-fitting, with the zipper open to the chest.

Those who don't know her well might think that her way of being is as transgressive and audacious as her appearance. Yet under that seemingly indestructible suit of armor, she hides a **tender and sensitive spirit, caring and considerate toward others** however discreetly she does it, respectful and never intrusive. Self-care, as she understands it, is undeniably a kind of protection against the outside world, a way of sheltering herself with that great sensitivity that sets her apart.

Among friends, she's fun and a total joy to be around, but when she's in a group, she moves back and forth from being exuberant and more extroverted and, in other moments, almost seeming to pull herself into the background, revealing an almost shy personality.

Her wardrobe is distinguished, obviously, by the presence of **clothes that are overtly sexy**: low-cut shirts, tight dresses, leather pants, and short coats. Animal prints are all over the place, both for clothes and for accessories.

And *all* her shoes are, clearly, equipped with **high heels**.

For her, there's really no reason for the reasonable heel to exist. Save for gym shoes, which she resigns herself to wear every so often (although she even wears these, if possible, with wedges) all the shoes in her closet have heels of at least ten to twelve centimeters. The only exception would be some summer sandals, the jeweled kind, which ensure sensuality even without the heel.

Leaving the house without being perfectly dressed and accessorized is unthinkable for the Sexy Woman. She can't even contemplate the possibility of just going out to the bakery without nail polish on or with her hair all frazzled in a mess.

While it may seem excessive to many others, this type of look gets, in reality, actually quite toned down and made much less awkward just from the way she's able to be so **friendly and down to earth**, making it easy to forgive her for showing herself at a wedding with such a vertiginously plunging neckline seemingly designed to make all the guests turn their attention to her cleavage.

When she's picking out her outfits, **she's almost never chasing after the latest trends**. She's well aware of what suits her and what brings out the best in her, and **there's no one who could convince her to wear something that doesn't fit her physique**.

For this reason specifically, she's inestimable on those days when friends get together to go shopping.

If you can get her to accompany you, you can rest easy that no salesperson, no matter how convincing, will ever be able to dump something on you that isn't perfect for you.

Plus, if you're looking for something for a romantic night, she most definitely will be able to find something that brings out your most sensual side in a flash.

While making her wardrobe decisions, she generally prefers **intense tones, stretch fabrics, and glittering transparencies**. She loves using lace as well, bringing together a seductive look with a more retro one.

The ability to wear sensual clothing with ease but also elegance constitutes the character of the Sexy Woman.

If wearing a jacket is a must, it will most likely be tight, short, and with a deep neckline, but if she's asked, she's capable of moderating and reining her outfit in, choosing some slightly less provocative pieces but no less understated because of it.

The tailoring and the cuts are all **pretty tight, but they are done wisely so as to mask any so-called imperfections** and to fully shine a spotlight on all her best qualities.

Blouses and sweaters can either be loose-fitting but with low-cut necklines (even in frigid weather, the Sexy Woman never gets a sore throat) or super skinny and very tight (always worn with the best push-up bra available).

Generally speaking, **she's well aware of what she wants to highlight, and she has crystal clear ideas about how to do it**. Thanks to this, if she's unable to find what she's looking for in the store or what would spice up her look the way she was hoping, she can make her own clothes—literally crafted to and for her body—from the fabrics and with the patterns she loves, with necklines, slits, and strategic openings exactly where and how she wants them to truly make her silhouette jump out.

Whenever she can, she makes extensive use of lace, from using it to show some skin on her daily outfits to entirely lace-made tube dresses popping with sensuality.

Even if she wears a pantsuit combo with a men's cut, she's still able to whip it into something immediately sexy with the addition of a lace top.

In those times when a more traditional outfit is called for, she's always able to demonstrate a simple sensuality thanks to her studied use of accessories.

Speaking of **accessories**, it should be pointed out that in this type of style, their use is usually limited in terms of quantity—so as to not draw attention away from her physique—but always **selected with extreme care**.

She rarely wears hats.

Her hair, a fundamental component of seduction, is typically loose and voluminous in all circumstances, and a pair of sizeable earrings with a particular form often further frames her face.

Gloves, once considered ripe with seductive power, are used much less these days—maybe for reasons of convenience, who knows?

The Sexy Woman will often choose bags with jewel-crowned finishes; however, it should be noted that on the scale of importance, they receive significantly less weight than shoes (the sensuality inherent to bags isn't such a developed idea, after all).

The date with the hairdresser is a sacrosanct moment, even if she doesn't go there all the time, considering that usually she prefers to wear her hair fairly long (even if, with age, this proclivity can change, evolving toward a shorter but still voluminous cut). **White hair is obviously unacceptable**, and for this reason she systematically resorts to DIY hair-dying maintenance, assuming that for some reason she's unable to find an appointment with her favorite stylist.

On the subject of makeup, her selection can vary a whole lot, generally depending on which aspects of her face she wishes to highlight. If she has deep-set eyes, there will be an abundance of mascara and eye shadow. However, if she prefers to draw attention to her mouth, then she'll opt for a flaming red tint, even at seven in the morning.

Needless to say, this type of look is outwardly eye-grabbing and **requires above all the capacity to remain unembarrassedly cool and unflappable when all eyes are on you**.

As noted before, though, this sensation gets softened and mitigated by the ease and the freshness that the Sexy Woman is able to muster when wearing the kinds of clothes that, for some women, would wind up being impossible to wear with even a sliver of nonchalance.

All this, coupled with an occasionally disarming candor, brings out a pleasant result, just shy of excessive.

It's a style and look that endows her with a note of **seduction** that, **flanked by the simplicity of her manners**, is one of the characteristics that sets her particular but undeniable *charme* apart from the rest.

How to Become a Woman of Charme

VI. The Sporty Woman: Classy Informality

Sandra is the pitch-perfect example of the Sporty Woman. The way that she is **pleasantly informal** in how she carries herself with an innate know-how gives her an admirable carefree attitude even in the most formal of occasions—**absolutely at ease and always with unique class**.

From an aesthetic point of view, we can say that she's the polar opposite of the Sexy Woman.

The clothes she chooses demonstrate a kind of classy informal style, **sporty but built for all seasons**, classic without being traditional. Her entire way of understanding how to care for her image, despite being relaxed and spontaneous, turns out to be an irreproachable example of how to dress no matter what the occasion.

At first glance, it might seem as though the Sporty Woman is more or less the same as the Informal Woman, seeing as there are a few similarities: informality above everything else, followed by spontaneity and the ability to feel at ease in every kind of situation, as well as to make those around feel equally at ease.

These two types of women, though, couldn't be any more different, because while the Informal Woman is imaginative and channels a more traditional style of femininity, the Sporty Woman **doesn't concern herself with too much creativity**, tapping into a more freewheeling *charme* and an open-ended interpretation of what femininity can be.

Flashy, attention-grabbing, or even just particular clothes are all but banished from her closet. The colors are almost exclusively neutral and kept to the usual suspects: grays, blacks, blues, browns, khakis, whites, and sometimes beiges. Loud colors and pastels (beloved by the Informal Woman) are extremely rare if not entirely absent.

On the whole, **she seems to relish rejecting the idea of the traditional feminine look**: the colors, patterns, fabrics, everything.

And yet, she still manages to exude an attractive sensuality that's every bit as strong as it is downplayed.

Contrary to what most would guess, underneath this more gender-neutral aspect lies a **sensitive character**, almost to a fault. If she sees someone suffering, she can't help dashing off to the rescue of those in need, brimming with the grit and energy that make her who she is. Far from being evidence of carelessness, her low-key demeanor is an asset that allows her to make herself heard always in the most thoughtful and measured of ways.

If you find her in a group, she's vivacious, compelling, enthusiastic, and never timid or afraid. She's a prime example of that classic kind of woman who **does an enormous amount of things and does it all with aplomb**. It's only among intimate friends that she reveals her vulnerability, her fears, her insecurities—all done with irresistible understatement.

No matter what informality she may dabble in, **her appearance is always cared for**. Her hair, usually short, is always well put-together, and the same goes for clothes, accessories, and outfits in general: **everything is in place**.

While picking out clothes exclusively hemming closer to the sportier, informal side of things (jeans, flat shoes, thick-heeled boots, sweaters, dress shirts, and blazers), she's still always expertly put-together and elegant, even in the most formal of environments. The elegance she lays claim to is one that only she knows how to obtain, composed entirely of **simple clothes that**

are linear and never too much, with which she cooks up an **outfit of impeccable class**.

Simple clothes with simple cuts, selected with impeccable taste, provide a classy outfit

From time to time, she decides to play around with more traditionally feminine forms like skirts and dresses: when she does this, her choices are linear patterns, never tight, often coupled with opaque tights and sporty scarves or ankle boots.

She uses **very little makeup** (sometimes none at all) and always with discretion. And yet she never fails to achieve a polished and careful presentation, even more so than many of her friends passing their days atop their high heels, decked out in tights and nail polish.

Fashion doesn't do much for her, so she rarely follows its trends that are too imaginative and eccentric for her style, notable for its extreme moderation, to say nothing of her avoidance of showy items of clothing and accessories.

But despite the apparently slight attention she gives to her look, if truth be told, she infallibly has good taste that helps her to always **grab the most perfect outfit possible for her physique without a second's hesitation**.

Color-wise, as we've noticed, neutral tones are the winners here.

As for fabrics, other than denim (used above all for jeans rather than shirts or jackets), she goes all in for fabrics that you're not likely to find in the women's department, while transparent, sumptuous, or iridescent textiles are obviously out of the question. Stretchy fabrics that show off her curves are also mostly unconsidered.

The cuts of her pants, shirts, and blouses are always airy, geometric, and impeccable.

She makes the most of **a small collection of clothes that is of the highest quality**. When one of these gets worn out, she seeks out another one just like it, unencumbered by the desire for novelty or variety. But all her outfits are perfectly selected and marvelously matched up, succeeding in appearing—just like her, of course—apropos for the situation at hand.

And if she wants, she knows how to pull off a surprising sexiness, even in a traditional pantsuit—jacket and all.

When it comes to **accessories**, she pares it down to the **essentials**. She doesn't, for example, own an infinite collection of shoes or dozens of bags or handbags.

Jewelry, assuming she wears any, is low in quantity and high in simplicity, meaning that junk jewelry is nonexistent. She'll bust out the hats, scarves, and gloves when it's cold, sure, but not as a complement to the outfit, and belts are only worn when necessary.

She has only one concession to make: her watch, which is often lovely and expensive.

Her knack for managing her wardrobe precisely reflects her character: **reasonable and rational, with little time to concern herself with frills**; she is **focused on the essential**.

This type of look, regardless of its apparent simplicity, isn't so easy to pull off, because the ability to pick out informal outfits with a sure hand, guaranteeing a result of pure class, is not something everyone possesses.

As we've pointed out, any woman who has this style can make herself **stand out thanks to her spontaneity and simplicity**, which brings together the wisdom of being able to put together the desired results in a natural way with apparently minimum effort; each detail is characterized by its linearity and sobriety while the whole number turns out to be incredibly sophisticated.

How to Become a Woman of Charme

VII. The Green Woman: Natural Simplicity

Linda is not your average kind of woman.

Reserved and sociable at the same time, she loves hearing about almost all the topics under the sun, and she's a passionate reader of anything and everything that gets into her hands: books, magazines, newspapers. Conversely, she hates television and tech gadgets in general.

Friendly and outgoing, hers is a direct and spontaneous *charme*, enough to make her seem **naive**.

When she's getting herself dressed—and at other times too—she favors light and natural colors that draw out her natural radiance and the brightness of her beautiful smile.

Her **love of nature and her respect for the environment** aren't fashionable hang-ups derived from eco trends so rampant these days—frequently more proclaimed with a loud voice than carried out in practice. Instead, they are both sincere and profound.

Having personal contact with nature is for her an enormous source of energy, a moment of replenishment.

Her interest in the environment is by no means a mannerism; it functions like a mirror for her whole approach to life. In order to avoid throwing the shopping list or the cookie wrapper into the trash for mixed waste collection, she'll keep it in her bag until she finds the right trash receptacle, or, more often, she'll hold onto it until she gets home, where she can drop it into the appropriate container. The result of this is that her bag usually verges on being the size of the trunk of a car.

Linda's style is clean and neat, just like her.
She tends to favor **natural fabrics** like cotton, silk, wool, hemp, and linen, wearing cuts that are simple and relaxed—she possesses that basic and essential simplicity that can only be obtained through an excellent sense of taste.

Plus, if she has the handicraft skills, she loves to create her own clothes, finding inspiration in the styles and patterns of the past and giving new life to fabrics no longer in vogue.

She rarely goes for bright colors and instead adores soft, natural tones, warm earth colors with hints of the indefinable shades of sand and stone, or the burnished brown of wood.

Fabrics like linen or hemp are usually left in their natural state, not dyed.

Jewelry of all kinds is held to a minimum or not worn at all.

Her **preference for vintage** also applies to bags and belts: if she is over thirty-five, she surely has items that she bought twenty or more years ago and continues to make the most of them with immense satisfaction.

The bags are usually capacious and roomy, built for holding onto all kinds of items as well as books, newspapers, and numerous pairs of glasses.

She prefers well-made **shoes with a low or even flat heel**, usually light or neutral leather in color.

She has the habit of coupling a knee-length skirt with flats, a combination not normally considered elegant but which, when worn by her, turns out to be pleasantly charming.

You'll rarely catch her in public in very dark colors (only in the winter) and never, ever in jeans.

Sometimes for slightly more formal outings, she'll toss on some more somber tones, lightening them up with some brighter accessories—a bone necklace, maybe.

*Natural colors with smooth and soft cuts and lines,
all of which compose the Green Woman's style*

Since the Green Woman tends to appreciate natural products that take care of her face without giving the impression of being made up, **makeup is reduced to a minimum and not very noticeable**. The only possible exception is a light veil of lipstick in tones paired well with her overall complexion.

Her hair is usually beautiful and thick. This is all thanks to the fact that, having never gotten into the use of perms, flat irons, and dyes (except for henna), she can count on always having a naturally splendid head of hair without needing any products or treatments.

Usually those who find themselves with this style opt for a cut that highlights the hair's fullness without requiring a great deal of work with brushes or hair dryers, which, although not unnatural, wouldn't really jibe with her easygoing appearance.

This style, definitely not suitable for everyone, boasts of being easily wearable during the summer and spring, when lighter colors prevail.

It could get a bit more difficult in the winter to make this look work, when the large-scale use of soft colors, paired with a complexion that's lost some color, can make the face appear pale or even tired. In this case, it's fundamental to take some precaution and mix in a scarf more in line with one's natural winter complexion to ensure that in contact with your face is a more defined color, or—as the Green Woman often does—try to spend part of the day in the open air in order to ensure a slightly tanned skin.

Moreover, **the use of natural colors is a considerable strong point** for three reasons.

First, all the natural colors contain a strong neutral component, and **they all match terrifically together**. So even if you don't have the best color-matching insight, you've already cleared the path for success, because each and every combination is the right one.

Secondly, the practice of using tones similar to one another has a **slimming effect** on the physique that can make the body seem visually taller, trimming and highlighting only what's been purposely highlighted.

Last, but definitely not least, when the skin is no longer as fresh as it once was, remember that your complexion can be revitalized and illuminated by wearing lighter and brighter tones, in contrast to the ubiquitous usage of black, which can harden the features and draw attention to wrinkles and worry lines.

So clearly the selection of natural and luminous colors constitutes a vitally important ally that Linda can wield to maximize her skin's luminosity while also softening her features to emphasize her characteristic expressivity.

One of the characteristics of this style is that it produces a **young, fresh, and relaxed image**, and it's a freshness that is born not out of the attempt to appear younger but rather from a **genuinely young and positive spirit**—and for this reason, it's absolutely authentic and vital.

How to Become a Woman of Charme

VIII. The Trendy Woman: fashion tailor-made

Noemi is a "modern woman."

She is always on the go and divides her time between work, home, family, and hobbies with high **energy and enthusiasm** that suggests she was born with the gift of ubiquity. Her more sedentary friends wonder how she manages to get everything done.

Having an **excited and passionate character, she throws herself into every activity head first**, joyfully savoring every new discovery. Extroverted and communicative, she loves talking all about herself and she is always in the spotlight. It is what makes her shine and what she likes the most.

Friends and acquaintances are enchanted by her and inexplicably genuinely interested in what *she* says, while—if *you* tried to do the same thing—after about half a minute you would find yourself silent and resigned to listening to, for the umpteenth time, the antics of little George.

Sociable and cheerful, **she transmits energy and enthusiasm**, and is therefore a real force of vitality for her friends of a calmer disposition.

In contrast to the Classic Woman, **she likes being the center of attention and getting noticed**. However, she does this not in a studied or forced way, but it comes naturally and freely to her, freeing her to be nice to all kinds of people from all walks of life.

Her bubbly inventiveness and liveliness, though, is only partially reflected in her way of understanding clothing and her image in general.

Being by nature a lover of all that is new, she is immediately taken by all the seasonal fashion innovations: it is precisely for this reason that she is most at risk of being an unwitting target of the most insidious ready-to-wear trends.

Her inexhaustible energy and her **love for change** often lead her to **follow the new trends when they first hit the market** but before they spread into a mass phenomena.

And so, even if unconsciously and often completely involuntarily, she scrupulously adopts new trends that parade down the catwalk, even if the new styles don't always suit her.

Luckily, her natural good fashion sense comes in handy and keeps her away from, in one period, buying an acid green puffy jacket or, in another, trying out some lilac streaks in her hair.

Additionally, her overwhelmingly enthusiastic character manages to make her garments seem well suited for her even if, upon closer inspection, they aren't at all.

She has a way of making trendy clothes seem original and exclusive, with results that are sometimes baffling but always very pleasing.

As for colors and patterns, what most interests her is the ability to **combine practicality with an imaginative and innovative look**.

This pairing of seeming opposites completes the ensemble with an impalpable, but always present, **charming feminine touch**—a blouse or a scarf with a particular texture or well-chosen makeup with striking nail polish can create an effortlessly charming look.

PART ONE: FINDING YOUR OWN STYLE

*The innate talent of the Trendy Woman in terms of
colors and striking patterns allows her to
anticipate the trends in what will soon become fashionable*

Denim is indispensable for Noemi, not only used in pants and jeans but also in other garments such as skirts, blouses, jackets, and sometimes handbags.

Also deeply loved and must-have are her leggings, usually combined with wraparound oversized sweaters.

In winter, she wraps herself in very warm lovely jackets that combine practicality and comfort with her alluring femininity, setting her apart from the rest.

Most likely you won't see her wearing outfits with a geometric or severe cut. However, she sometimes wears garments she modified on her own: often her unerring instinct leads her to **anticipate the trends instead of following them**, and then, if she doesn't find what she is looking for, she manages to adjust the clothes herself, with unexpected and very pleasant results.

As for **footwear**, she obviously adores fashionable gym shoes and **sneakers** that are a little less sporty, and she has them in an **infinite number of colors and patterns** that can be combined, according to the occasion, with belts or other accessories.

In the winter months, she prefers to wear low-heeled knee-high boots in combination with her favorite pair of jeans or a short skirt with heavy tights, adding to her signature practical and yet very feminine look.

She generally avoids thin heels, especially during the day. Considering all the activities that she does in a given day, it seems inappropriate to get it all done in stilettos.

The use of accessories reflects her character and mood; she is more animated and inspired when she feels more effervescent, and they become subdued when her routine makes her tired or when she has some work to do that particularly bores her.
Her bags are usually large with a curved shape and soft texture, either in leather or fabric.
She wears fanciful and lively jewelry in a carefree way that never seems excessive.
Her gloves and scarves are usually versatile and lend themselves to being quickly matched to any outfit, even when leaving the house in a rush.

As for **makeup and hair**, she is the ideal customer for every hairdresser and beautician because of her love for the new and **desire to experiment with different things**, which is always great fun.

Her choices range from one outfit to another, with enormous versatility. Usually, however, she has a habit of creating two distinct looks: one for day that is marked by convenience, and one for evening, when eccentricity prevails.
And so, if by day she wears a practical ponytail combined with a touch of gloss, we can be certain that by night she'll be out

flaunting her playful side with colored eye shadow and elaborate hairstyles.

Her imagination and practicality, together with her femininity and her enthusiasm, which she uses to face every moment of the day, create a unique and outstanding ensemble in which her look reflects the characteristics that distinguish her personality in every way.

Her look, like her, is **whimsical, striking, communicative, and joyful**, and it transmits, above all, **an overwhelming surge of energy**.

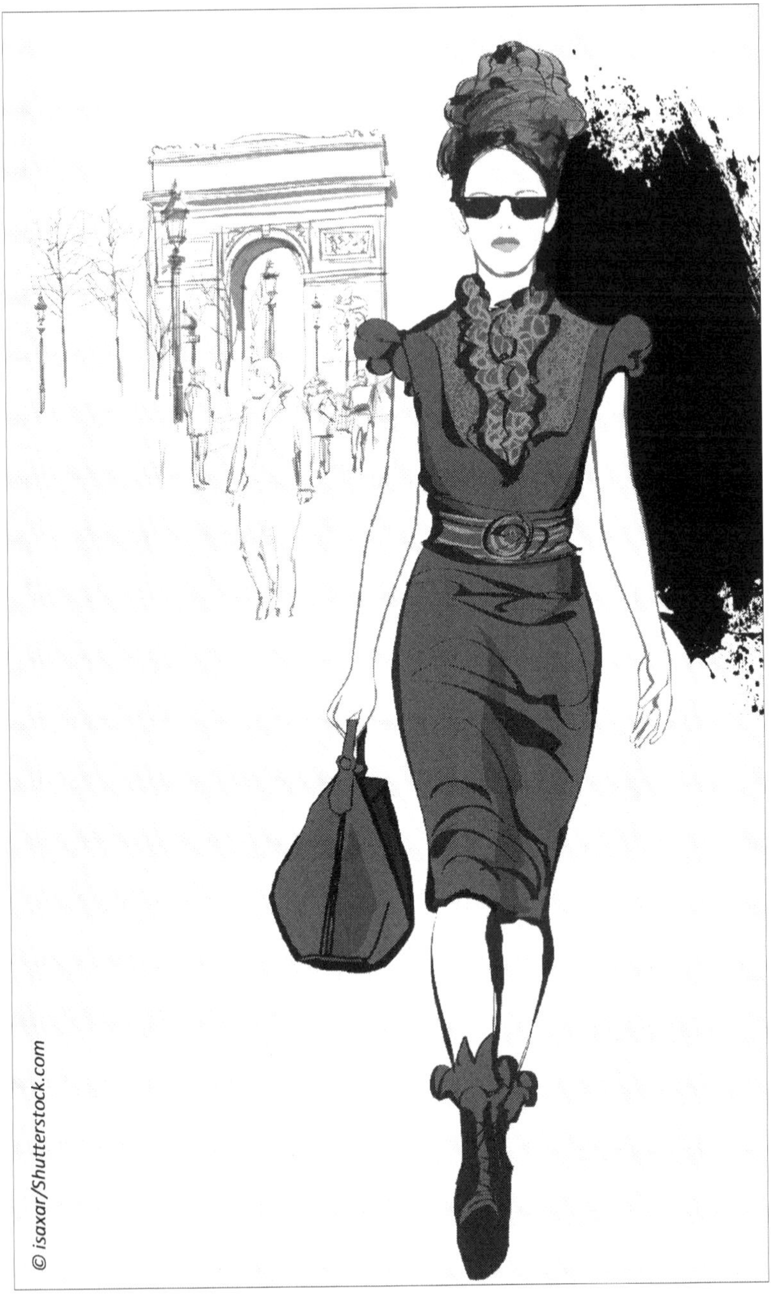

IX. The Artistic Woman: Creative and Unconventional

Allegra is the perfect example of the Artistic Woman. Full of energy, she is a veritable volcano erupting with ideas, not only for herself but also for others.

She can always suggest where to go, what to do, where to find a particular object, and how to spend a weekend that is out of the ordinary.

She brings **passion and enthusiasm** to everything she does and spreads it to others.

Even if she's a curvy woman in the prime of her life, she likes to say, "Wherever I go, men look at me," sometimes causing a certain wry smile from her younger female friends. But when you spend time around her, try to simply observe her walking down the street from a distance, and you will see that men actually are turning and craning their necks to look at her. Even if she doesn't have jaw-dropping plunging necklines, knockout legs, or long flowing hair, what she does possess is **an undeniable and unique *charme***.

Her wardrobe is characterized by a **mix of fairly standard and special clothes**, which are absolutely always successfully combined in the most appropriate way with good taste.

Depending on the place and occasion, sometimes she prefers more eccentric outfits (intense colors and particular items that perfectly match each other), while from time to time she may use classic shades such as gray, white, beige, and black that are enlivened by **some eye-catching accessory that never becomes excessive on her**.

You'll never see her in a pantsuit, nor in a formal evening dress.

Yet when she wants, and when the occasion demands it, she can be incredibly elegant, always with **a touch of flair that sets her apart** from other women.

She is able to cleverly blend garments together that, when separated, would seem anonymous and banal, resulting in an extraordinary, unmistakably special, and unconventional overall effect. You can almost say that her fashion sense becomes a mirror of her character and mood that she uses to transmit her **volcanic and overwhelming personality**.

The cuts she likes are rather like her: lose yet sensual, all-embracing but strong.

She likes to layer clothes, such as form-fitting classic leggings with slightly oversized sweaters. Eccentric scarves, necklaces, or bracelets—specially made, sometimes even by herself—complete this look of hers that is never flashy or in poor taste.

She often combines lightweight fabrics with key textiles made from a substantially dense weave, some of which seem like artistic masterpieces thanks to the combinations of yarns and weaves.

She loves **authentically vintage fashion** that she fishes out of her mother's, grandmothers', and aunts' wardrobes, pairing these items with contemporary attire, resulting in absolutely unusual but tasteful combinations.

Even when she happens to wear seemingly classic and traditional clothes, such as a jacket and a pencil skirt, she always manages to look special, different, and oh so pleasantly unconventional.

Due to her natural talent and skills, she often dabbles in making some small but clever changes to her clothes that make them more special and personalized, even if they started out completely bland.

The choice of interesting accessories, combining extravagance and character, leads to wildly diverse outfits in perfect harmony for the Artistic Woman

Even **her use of colors reveals her soul as an artist**: she successfully unites various vibrant tones together with a completely harmonious result. Typically, **she shies away from pairing tone on tones**, which is typical of more traditional styles, as we have seen in the previous pages. With a liberal use of gray, she can effortlessly blend complementary colors, avoiding an overly lit effect.

The choice of bright colors for her entire image, however, is usually reserved for special occasions. For her daily wardrobe, she usually prefers neutral tones with the addition of a single bright-colored garment or a particular accessory.

The use of **accessories** in this kind of style, as we have seen, is **abundant and imaginative while always staying tasteful**.

The necklaces, brooches, and bracelets she wears are extravagant and eccentric, often made with unusual or recycled materials. She favors belts that aren't necessarily made from traditional materials, such as leather, and are instead most often made from scarves or invented with uncommon and playful materials.

Shoes and bags are good quality and may sometimes be eccentric. Even in this case, when it's possible, she chooses vintage items.

Gloves and scarves, usually combined with one another, can be of a traditional or a decidedly eccentric cut and color, depending on the combination with the rest of the outfit: bright colors on monochrome ensemble or neutrally toned garments on top of a wild color.

The hats the Artistic Woman casually wears vary in colors and patterns. She likes a real note of color on gray rainy days so as not to go unnoticed, even under an umbrella.

As for **makeup**, her tendencies are exactly the opposite. Her inventiveness in her choice of clothing and accessories is transformed into simplicity regarding makeup, which is **limited to what helps enhance her mouth, eyes, and complexion without any eye-catching element**, revealing once again her own personal and innate good taste. Her day-to-day makeup, depending on her mood, can pass as being natural and low-key one day and more sophisticated on another day. Sometimes she uses a moderately brighter color for lipstick, although quite rarely for eye shadow, but of course her use of color is never showy or out of place.

As for her **hairstyle**, she generally **avoids a regular cut** as well as the smoothed hair obtained with a hair dryer and brush. However, she takes care of her hair meticulously with the help of her trusted hairdresser, who knows her and knows what hairstyle enhances her explosive personality. Unexpectedly, she sometimes lets her hair grow out so that she can collect it into a very traditional bun that, on her, becomes kind of an unconventional and innovative hairstyle.

As for color, we see instead two diametrically opposite inclinations: at a young age, she sometimes likes to have hair with flair, and she may experiment with many different colors, as if her head were a canvas to paint on.

When fifty years have passed, however, she rarely chooses to dye her hair, because she considers the dye as something inauthentic and not in line with her character. So when her hair begins to turn gray, she often decides to let it be natural, perhaps enhancing its tone with a slightly lighter contrast, yet her positive and enthusiastic character and her awareness that **lighter hair softens her features** and enhances her face enable her to remain **fresh and youthful with the passing years**.

This kind of style, as you may imagine, is not suitable for everyone. It presupposes a nonconformist and **unconventional personality**, an unstoppable creative streak, and **a very strong character**.

However, **even women with a generally conservative character can take up this style for short periods**—for example, during a time of intense change. Each and every one of us can turn to this style when we feel the desire for a breath of fresh air and there is **a need to break the mold, even if it's not for long**—perhaps just for a vacation, or maybe just for one evening.

Try to experience it, if you want. It may not be the style that suits you, and you might only adopt it for a short period of time. But the simple fact of having experienced it will help you look at everything—from your look to your life—in a new way.

It'll enrich your style, whatever it may be.

X. Extremes to Avoid: Fashion Victim, Overbranded, and Alternative to the Bitter End

FASHION VICTIM

Tatiana is a fun and happy woman. She loves being in the company of others and she's a good friend; she is lively but dependable.

On the surface of things, she demonstrates to those around her a very social and expansive way of being, but her outer personality hides a hint of insecurity, a **lack of faith in her own taste**.

Although she always wishes to be ahead of the curve of fashion trends, she also tends to be **afraid of making her own choices**, so—out of a combination of fear and laziness—she looks for the things that are most in vogue without giving any consideration as to whether they comprise a look that's suitable for her.

For example, if the color highlighter yellow is trendy, she will enthusiastically snatch up all the clothes in town dominated by that color...without considering that maybe it isn't the best for showing off her curves or that it doesn't pair well with her complexion.

After a few months, she'll find herself with a closet full of less-than-satisfying clothes because everything is already out of style, not to mention not right for her physique. This leads to the great idea that she now needs to buy more items.

But once again, timorous and afraid of her own good taste, she slavishly goes on **grabbing everything she sees featured in the magazines** or on the mannequins in the boutique windows.

In the end, she's left with the same result and the same dissatisfaction as the year before.

In addition to this, there's also the fact that in continuously renewing her wardrobe, she ends up **spending a shocking amount of money every season**, and this usually **prevents her from investing in high-quality fabrics** that are more expensive but long-lasting. Her choices frequently are cut down to less-than-great fabrics or clothes with really imperfect cuts. And so she winds up distancing herself via these choices even further away from the well-manicured look she was hoping for.

Where Tatiana really goes afoul in her approach, as each one of us can imagine, is in **losing any stylistic personalization**, leaving her with a poorly defined look.

From garments to accessories, but also from makeup to the cut and color of the hair, **every choice she makes is based on what's hot at the moment**, without giving any consideration to what's really personally figure-flattering or what meshes with her personality.

Depending on the trends, her not exactly straight legs end up wearing a miniskirt or body-hugging skinny jeans, or if she has ample cleavage she may end up completely hiding it underneath large shirts buttoned up to the neck, as long as the trends say so.

Dyes and hairstyles are chosen with stunning disregard for the complexion, the shape of her face, or what would work the best on her given her personality.

It should go without saying that **the turnout is a little bit disappointing**. And yet, if we look around, we can see that what she's wearing is a response to a significantly diffuse trend, and what's more this trend repeats itself over time.

What can we do in these cases?

The remedy is as simple as it is pleasant to put into practice: *trust your instincts* rather than the glossy magazines!

After all, when you buy a fuchsia puffy coat with cheeks of matching color thanks to the frigid winter air, you pretty much *know* you're going to regret it. But the compliments of the salesclerk and the images seen on TV are so temptingly convincing that they win over your natural and very sensible concern, and you finish the day by finding yourself with one more useless piece of clothing in your closet and fifty fewer dollars.

So *use your head*!

Don't give a damn about what your friends are wearing.

Enjoy the fashion shows and runways as though they are wonderful documentaries about costume history, not model standards to copy.

Read the magazines, sure, but with **a little bit of a critical perspective**.

Pick out your clothes by looking at *your own* colors, not the models'.

Trust in this: the optimal results will come flying in.

OVERBRANDED

Virginia is a reserved, almost shy person. A good listener, she's always been fearful of the judgment of others and has always shown little interest in putting herself out there.

She has little trust in her own capabilities, and paradoxically she surrounds herself with people who continually criticize her for what they think she's lacking, which only contributes to and balloons her insecurities.

Her slightly timid nature also shows itself in the choices she makes for her look; **she's always trying to find some point of reference that will make her feel more confident**.

Completely opposite to Tatiana, **she doesn't follow any contemporary trends—they're too shifty**, not giving her the confidence she's after.

Instead, she's always on the lookout for the most expensive brands, regardless of whether any given piece may be high quality or in good taste or not.

For her, brands are almost an untouchable necessity, giving her a sense of confidence and providing her with the criteria she needs to make her choices, regardless of the actual quality of the garment or how it looks on her.

She's an assiduous regular at all the sales and is on the ever-continuing search for the best opportunity—because designer clothes, as you know, charge a pretty penny for the label—invariably purchasing unsold leftover stock, clothes that have gone unsold because they feature colors or patterns of dubious taste or that fashion has already passed by and now nobody wants any longer.

For hairdressers and beauticians, she relies on the most well-known name. Inevitably, she winds up disappointed despite the huge figure appearing at the bottom of her receipt.

And so, despite her earnest desire to appear put together and refined, she always has **a worn-out look that is quite out of step with the times**, which then exacerbates her already fearful nature and lack of self-confidence, triggering a vicious cycle that's really difficult to get out of.

Once again, in this case, the solution is simple enough.

All she has to do is essentially invert her canon of references—**seek out *quality*, not just name brands**.

Have fun hunting for the most sophisticated fabrics, even if there is no brand name on them.

Take an interest in the history of each yarn—its origins, how it's manufactured. In no time at all, you'll be able to recognize, without a moment's hesitation, a high-quality piece of clothing, and you'll able to make your future choices based on that rather than brand.

Try to find the hairstyle that screams *you* the most in old magazines and in books, and propose that style to your hairdresser instead of walking around with a head of hair that bears your stylist's signature touch but which seems to have been designed for a head that isn't *yours*.

If you really must have a brand, let it be your own.

What you'll see is that in no time at all, you'll be making your own trends, and this will be oh so much more fun.

ALTERNATIVE UNTIL THE BITTER END

Lara is the quintessential Alternative Woman. She shuns brands, trends, and the dominant fashions, but rather than doing so out of natural inclination (like the Informal Woman or the Artistic Woman, who are nonconformist by nature), her behavior is based on pure choice—so much so that **she would never, ever take home a fashionable piece of clothing**, even one that is the most suitable color and pattern for her, just because.

Intelligent and well informed, her bulwark is the act of being different, yet sometimes she's definitely too rigid about it, and this doesn't in any way add to her *charme* or her femininity.

In her own way, she's also extremely subject to the sways of fashion—through negation rather than acceptance. But don't you dare tell her that, because it would really make her furious.

As a matter of fact, she's always on the hunt for things that are decidedly *not* fashionable, that *don't* give off the impression of being looked after, that seem spontaneous and unsophisticated. But since they're all the fruits of a deeply meticulous search, they're not that spontaneous at all, and you can see it all too well.

Her clothes are scruffy, but it's a studied carelessness, not a natural one.

Both hair and makeup are reduced to a minimum, if not entirely missing.

She seems to think that giving too much thought to these things is a sign of superficiality, and so even in the most formal situations, she cultivates a studiously casual look, making herself appear sloppy and even lacking in respect for those around her.

This type of approach to image—which is a kind of pseudo-*disinterest* in image—is **completely counterproductive**, as obvious as that may be.

Beyond being an aesthetically harsh look, this mentality shows a clear trend in which **carelessness becomes a sort of mark of pride, a denial of one's femininity**, almost as if being a woman was something to move on from, not something to celebrate.

Not taken into consideration is the fact that self-care and taking care of those around you is a way of emphasizing your own personality, *not* something that dims your shine.

Inverting this inclination won't be easy, because its origins are sunk way down with some profoundly deep roots that cannot just be yanked out—certainly not just by reading this book.

Nevertheless, there's one consideration from all this that might be useful. The idea of not being a slave to the trends, of always being different from everyone else—you can't just stumble onto this approach out of carelessness. Instead, you end up with a style that is, in its own way, preapproved, because it's ordinary enough across all the people who think like you, and there are more of them than you think.

Instead, **differentiating yourself thanks to your own good taste and femininity**, trying to bring out the most of your unique characteristics, **is much more interesting**.

Try it, just for fun, even if it's just to show yourself that you can indeed do something new. You'll soon find that it's nothing short of inspiring.

PART TWO

The Practical Rules of Charme

XI. Rules and Personality

*Elegance doesn't mean being noticed,
it means being remembered.*
—Giorgio Armani

Talking about rules in terms of *charme* can seem contradictory. Of course, *charme*, as we have already seen, should present itself naturally rather than coming off as studied or rehearsed.

So, you might be wondering, if style is supposed to arise instinctively from our own taste and personality, why even talk of "rules"?

The answer is logical: it is because **each style, however innate and unplanned it may be, has a purely aesthetic and visual impact**. For this reason it is not surprisingly called *image*. Although this term might seem superficial, its meaning is much deeper than just appearance, as it reflects the way we relate to others as well as ourselves.

Visual impact is necessarily influenced by the existing **relationships among**, for example, **different colors, geometric proportions of clothes** and accessories, **and physical characteristics of our own figure**.

The rules that we are speaking about in this chapter are therefore not in any way dogmas to follow. They are simply suggestions on considering our approach to color, the differences between fabrics, and **how to enhance our figure and bring out our best qualities**. Then, depending on our preferred style, there will always be the option of following these suggestions or not, depending on the desired effect, our character, and our mood at the moment.

Proportion of clothing is incredibly important in order to mask any imperfections, all while celebrating out strong points

The rules that we will see in the following pages, then, are simply technical instructions that can be played with in a way that suits each personality, body, and occasion. The rules fall under several categories:

•**Colors**: our choice of color should be a strategic way of enhancing our eyes, skin, and hair in order to help us always look our best. We will see together how, by changing the color of even a single article of clothing, not only can you make the whole outfit pop and obtain the most suitable look for you, but it can also help you express your character and improve your mood when you need it!

•**Patterns**: this aspect of clothes is fundamental to bringing out the best in our body type, hiding what we do not like about it. The patterns on the garments, and in some cases even on accessories, are subject to rules of proportion that can change perceptions of how we look. These are rules that everyone should know how to use to their advantage, and knowing these rules can also allow you to break or modify them, if you want to!

- **Textiles**: every fabric is the result of a particular manufacturing process, craft or industrial. Learning about the origin and meaning of cloth is an element that helps give character and uniqueness to our style.

- **Accessories**: this is a vast subject that could take whole books to talk about in a comprehensive manner. In the next few pages, we'll try to briefly cover how they complement different styles and how they can be combined with various outfits, creating unfailing and flawless combinations.

- **Occasions**: they represent an extremely broad topic of great importance for all styles, whether it is the daily choice of outfit or the clothing selection for unique events.

- **Organization of the wardrobe**: this might seem like a trivial subject and could even seem irrelevant in terms of style. However, it represents the necessary balance of the previous topics by allowing us to improve the practical management of our space and the time that we dedicate to our look. When we reorganize our closet, we can easily avoid the huge dispersion of precious energy that could otherwise be used for more interesting activities.

The goal, as we'll see, is to match our very authentic style with our personality, recalling Coco Chanel's quote: "Dress shabbily and they remember the dress; dress impeccably and they remember the woman".

XII. Colors:
The Nuances of *Charme*

(Note: some images in the black-and-white edition have been removed, primarily in chapter XII, "Colors". These images can be found on my blog, www.ladonnadicharme.it, or in the e-book version, which can be downloaded on any smartphone, tablet, or PC.)

In every place and occasion, the use of different tones and nuances of color play **a key role in defining our style**.

We could even argue that colors easily represent the most noticeable aspect of our outfit, the highlights that identify us and make us uniquely our own. In a certain sense, color is the first thing we put on; it's that certain something that articulates the characteristics of our look.

Worth remembering, however, is the fact that the role of color boils down to **two different aspects**, both equally important.

The first and most easily understandable approach to color is **how to pick out the right color given the combination of different accompanying colors**—a red sweater, for example, is totally different from an identical sweater in white. Generally speaking, this is the way most people go about choosing the appropriate colors for their outfits.

The second item to consider is something that has been gaining more and more importance in recent years and is often featured in magazines and on blogs, and that is **the pairing relationship between a specific tint or hue with the colors of our eyes, hair, and skin**. The combination doesn't end there, though, and also includes **our physical forms**, such as curvy, thin, short, and so on.

Usually, this aspect is only apparent for the strongest combinations and colors. For example, blond hair is enhanced by a midnight-blue sweater, a tanned complexion is emphasized by a white dress, and so on. But in reality this applies to all kinds of colors and shades, especially the soft, delicate ones that, contrary to what you'd think, have a drastically different effect on each one of us.

Before we can even think intelligently about what colors go together, it's absolutely fundamental to identify the effects of different tints and hues with respect to our own personal complexions. This is especially true for those articles of clothing that are worn close to the face.

Providing a clear description is by no means easy because there are infinite possible ways of matching clothing color with your hair/eyes/complexion, and besides, **you can't describe a color in words**—a slight difference in its hue can completely change its effect.

By and large, though, we can generally trust a simple rule that is easy enough to follow: we must **determine if our predominant colors are warm or cold and emphasize them with a complimentary tonality**, tossing aside those that would be too similar. For example, beige typically doesn't give a whole lot of love to those with a more olive complexion, because it brings out the dark circles under the eye or signs of tiredness, while for someone with a rosier complexion, beige really works well. This is similar to how a bottle-green type of color will be perfect for a woman who has hair and tones with some coppery streaks, while it would be disastrous for an ash-blond woman, in whose hair the more dominant, colder tones prevail. And so it's in this way that gray, a perfect match for a honey-blond woman, instead gets flattened if paired with someone who has ice-blond hair.

An easy trick to choose the best color for you is to stand in front of a mirror close to a window (natural light always helps you see your colors better) trying on clothes of the most different colors and hues to discover which tones enhance your colors in the best way possible.

And before you get upset, remember that even if there is a color that you're particularly crazy about but which just isn't your perfect color, there are still so many ways to use it—accessories, skirts, or pants, for example, all with huge effect. **Even just adding a scarf in a hue that suits you the most** can help bring out all the best colors in your face.

As to the use of colors for a recognizable and attractive style, it can be risky to rely on only the colors that are in vogue at the moment. This is especially true if accompanied by the all too ubiquitous black, a combination that can turn out a little banal, if not overly thought out.

Much more interesting would be to **consider the most popular and trendiest of colors only as sources of inspiration**, something that can be used to figure out how to match in originally creative ways.

For another example, let's think about **the true classic colors**, in particular **some of the master Renaissance painters**, all of them outstanding exemplars in choosing **extraordinary and timeless combinations that are as eternally eye-catching** as their fame. Be sure to give a look not only at the foreground figures but also the background, the decorations, the landscapes, and the buildings. You'll find color solutions that will be unique, original, and classic, all at the same time, which will add inspiration to your daily outfits as well as those reserved for fancier, more particular moments.

If you want to have a breathtaking and definitely gorgeous look, the suggestion is to *have fun* with colors, experimenting with new shades at all times, finding excitement also in **the infinite variety of the more "neutral" colors**.

These shades, depending on the situation, can be emphasized by what we can call colorful **"accent elements,"** juxtaposed against the more neutral ones. One of the secrets of giving new life to a slightly monochrome outfit, or one with a more tone-on-tone matching relationship, is to throw in a more intense complimentary color, guaranteeing you a to-die-for chic result that's a little bit out of the ordinary.

Using accented colors emphasizes the garments by giving a personal note to the whole outfit

For example, an accessory with yellow or orange tones will pop in an outfit dominated by blue (especially denim blue), just as dark tones will be illuminated by bright colors (gray and yellow for instance).

COLORS AND STYLE

As for the pairings, let's keep in mind that in general **every style distinguishes itself in its own way of matching and**

coupling all the colors, as we've pointed out in the first part of the book.

The **Informal Woman**, for example, will prefer simple but harmonious combinations, typically based on the pairing of intense colors with some of the more timeless shades like denim and black, plus white in the summer months.

Conversely, the **Classic Woman** will tend to choose more or less dark or traditional colors such as blue, bottle green, brown, or Bordeaux—often splashed with new vivacity thanks to other colorful articles. Gray is also frequently deployed, both on its own in all of its nuances and matched against pastels in the summer as well as with livelier colors in the winter.

The **Sophisticated Woman** will have the time of her life playing around with all the colors that go well with blue, white, or beige. The timeless white, red, and blue combination is one of her go-to specialties, as well as some more understated shades of beige and gray combined with each other and often spiced up with some accent colors. And camel, with its warm tint falling somewhere between orange and brick, is one of the most classic and all-purpose accent colors for accessories.

As we've seen earlier, the **Sexy Woman** takes full advantage of all the uses of black, the color often considered to be the queen of all the sexiest colors, but she also makes good use of animal prints. In the warmer months, she digs out the bright colors and wears them from head to toe, carefully crafting her outfits according to her physique and her skin and hair tones, always with the objective of grabbing attention.

The **Sporty Woman** relies on neutral and subdued colors, usually combined with black or gray. She usually snatches up jeans whose blue hue is almost a neutral one, as well as making use of black or gray denim. The use of pastels is totally avoided; she would rather cut off an arm than wear a *pink* sweater.

Moving on to the **Green Woman**, light and muted tones are her preferred standbys, slightly pastel at times but almost unnoticeably, with beiges and warm earth tones comprising the rest of her most loved colors. Obviously, preference is given to those with natural dyes that have a subtle and soft effect.

By her very nature, the **Trendy Woman** will pair the most vogue color of the moment, preferably bright, with a pair of jeans, incorporating an ample use of black both in the clothing as well as in the accessories.

Even more diverse are the choices of the **Artistic Woman**, who'll alternate grays and muted tones, apart from the more obvious black, with bright and luminous colors flowing in accord with her logic, always unpredictable.

But on a more general level, whatever style you happen to choose, you can easily get a pleasing result, refined but particularly brought together, by doing two things: first, **picking out a base color and toying with its infinite nuances** and variations, and secondly, **finding the complementary color to work with the former**, which is basically what's on the other side of the first color's position on the color wheel.

Here is a good moment to remember that more creative stylizations, while requiring a greater sense of stylistic foresight, allow for a much wider range of possibilities and can turn otherwise ordinary ideas into phenomenal pairings.

THE NEUTRALS

To further expand upon the limitless possibilities offered by the careful use of color, another bit of wisdom would be to dig into the huge spectrum of **neutral colors**, which offer a nearly **infinite possibility of choices**. These middle ground colors give us the opportunity to really go wild with unexpected combinations, allowing us to achieve results that set themselves apart from the more traditional approaches to fashion, characterized by **that one extra touch that becomes the recognizable trademark of your style**.

Right here, perhaps, would be a good place to briefly describe just what we mean by neutral colors and, in general, how color perception works.

It's not so easy to explain how to single out the different tones, because our perception of a specific color changes completely depending on the other surrounding colors, as you can see in the image below.

The perception of a certain color changes depending on the surrounding hues: the two small squares look different, but they are exactly the same color!

For this reason, **combining different tones can really be an exciting process**. It can produce different and immensely satisfying results every time, becoming an essential tool for creating a unique outfit.

The colors that can be paired easily with one another, contrary to what you might think, aren't necessarily those that represent variations in lightness and darkness of the same tone. **The most harmonious and elegant combinations are found in all the colors we've defined as neutral**, because their original color is less immediately recognizable.

Looking at **the hues where the original tone is attenuated and no longer easily recognizable** can help us spot out the neutral colors, or the universal colors that can easily match with any other tone.

To be clear, this is not in any way about pale, undefined, or flat colors with little character, but rather intense tints to which the addition of the main neutrals (black, white, gray) have rendered the starting colors almost unrecognizable, allowing a much more fluid and immediate matching potential.

Even with intense tints like red, bright green, or lemon yellow, **a touch of gray is all you need to add to bring about a deep, proper transformation of the base tone**—more malleable, less hard, and phenomenally more disposed to being paired with other colors.

An admirable example of using neutral tones, leading to a refined and very chic outfit

Besides, neutral tones are the ones that allow us to find the colors that seem most built for us individually, for our complexion or our physique or for the occasion, but also for our mood, equipping us with one more tool to bring out our most glamorous glow.

And obviously, the greater the presence of black, gray, or white, the more impactful this transformation will be. For example, bright red can become a super elegant bordeaux or an enchanting brown, as well as including all the magnificent shades between these two colors. Cotton candy pink becomes a captivating aged pink, hot yellow becomes warm ochre, purple becomes a sumptuous plum or mauve, and on and on.

The most fascinating aspect of neutral colors is that each is different from the next, as noted earlier. **Each is able to take on practically infinite combinations.** Once a color has become neutral, it only becomes easier to match it up with all others.

Conversely, **combinations of pure colors are much riskier and much more attuned to decidedly nonconformist styles**—for example, the Artistic Woman first and foremost, but also the Informal Woman and both the Sexy and Trendy Woman, all of whom will no doubt find these experiments thrilling.

Another use of neutral colors, ready-made for all styles and occasions, is also adding to a monochromatic outfit (even with bright colors) **neutral-toned accessories and details, choosing among cool hues** (white gloves, gray bag, ice shoes) **or warm hues** (leather-colored shoes, ochre bag, camel gloves).

Without appearing too flashy, the result of this method is a really casual look with the whole outfit transmitting a sensation of harmony and elegance, enchanting with its impalpable *charme.*

XIII. Patterns and Shapes: The Secret of Proportion

A dress should be tight enough to show that you're a woman, but loose enough to prove that you're a lady.
—Edith Head

As every woman knows well, a dress can **shape, slenderize, thin, and hide things you want hidden**, emphasize the ones you want celebrated, **and even make us seem taller or shorter**.

We can use clothes to make the most not only of our physique but also of our faces: with careful attention to colors and fabrics, it's also possible to emphasize the luminosity of our hair or skin, and obtain a fresh and rested aspect.

Think about it: **just by changing one simple piece of clothing or a pair of accessories, the whole outfit can become something totally different**. A spot-on choice will by necessity wind up not only making us revel in our beauty but also rendering our daily activities a bit more pleasant, thanks to the fact that we feel comfortably at ease.

So we've got to ask: what are the guidelines to isolating what is most suitable for our bodies?

Just as in the previous chapter, the first thing to keep in mind is that **clothes don't necessarily have to be elegant, expensive**, or polished, but they do have to **adapt themselves to the characteristics of the person wearing them**. This rule of adaptability should also apply to the activities that we have planned for the day, but this is another topic, and we'll take a closer look at it in the following chapters.

The first step we have to take is **pointing out which elements about ourselves we'd like to make stand out and which ones we'd like to maybe draw attention away from**, at which point we can decide what allows us to accomplish this best.

MAKING THE MOST OF OUR STRONG POINTS

To begin, let's take a peek at a list of the **rules of geometry** that can be **applied to what some people would consider to be "imperfections,"** even if they're really not that at all: too full-figured, too thin, too short, and so on. In part, this relates to much of what we've seen in the previous chapter on the use of colors, showing that the use of one color over another is capable of modifying even the perception of your form.

With that in mind, it's crucial to be aware that, in general, **whatever you may consider an "imperfection" is usually accompanied by something to be enriched** and enhanced.

A full-figured body, for example, is usually accompanied by an ample bust begging to be highlighted by low necklines and daring cuts. Thus, **utilizing clothes with a less defined cut**—or even without a form at all—**to flatten out any extra pounds is completely counterproductive**, because it doesn't give you the opportunity to emphasize those shapely strong points that a slightly curvier woman is blessed with.

Among other things, **the feeling of carrying around a few more pounds than you'd like** is more often than not an entirely subjective concern **and frequently doesn't correspond whatsoever to reality**. I have many friends who always choose shapeless clothes because they are convinced they are overweigh; while, when they wear more form-fitting clothes, they reveal lovely physiques.

Moreover, today is it very simple to find at very reasonable prices these so-called **shaping linens** and fabrics that allow you to cut off centimeters where you'd like to as well as provide curves in the areas where you'd love to see some. Why rob ourselves of this opportunity?

Clothes purposefully cut with the idea of **shaping and highlighting your curves instead of covering them can get you feeling beautiful, attractive,** and perfectly at ease in every situation.

So here are some suggestions that you can apply to achieve your desired effect.

TO APPEAR A BIT THINNER

- ✓ For those who for whatever reason believe they have a few extra pounds around the **waistline**, clothes with a **straight cut** are typically fine, since women with this physique typically have thin legs and arms. Keeping the waistline unseen and **leaving the legs and the arms visible** creates a slimming effect on the figure.

© filitova/Shutterstock.com

High-waisted clothes or clothes with strategic layers render the hips and the waist invisible, enhancing legs and arms

- ✓ A similar result can also be attained with long sweaters cut quite wide around the bust combined with **tight skirts and pants that draw attention to the slimmer points** of the figure while not emphasizing the waist.

- ✓ If it's your **hips** that you're worried about, remember that in most cases a pair of close-fitting pants can work some magic on them while maintaining their form. On the other hand, picking out **a pair of large pants has the effect of enlarging your whole figure**.

- ✓ For those who'd like to camouflage a few pounds hanging around the waistline without resorting to broad cuts, the strategic use of **pleats** can help tremendously: the volume is still there, but everyone thinks that it's because of the pleats of the fabric rather than anything else!

- ✓ Additionally, there's a cut that works wonders for every body; perhaps surprisingly, it is even a total knockout for curvier women, slimming and harmonizing their forms in just the right places. We're talking about a cut that resembles the shape of a wedding dress, or even a frock coat, with its **vertical cuts and the wider width of the skirt but without frills that give a ballooning impression**, this cut reduces and slims the waist. If you are on the bustier side, you can highlight this feature with a beautiful V-neck. One more trick for those who don't have a waistline as slim as they'd like is to never wear a belt. It's a horizontal cut that divides the figure and widens the waist, so it's best to use it wisely.

- ✓ For those who, despite having wider womanly hips or strong legs, are lucky enough to have a **narrow waistline**, one way to maximize this is with **amphora-shaped cuts**. Those who have this figure, for example, look perfect in a really feminine skirt, gathered at the waist, which gives a very retro 1950s look. This suggestion is also suitable for women who instead have narrow hips and want more feminine curves.

✓ If you wish to appear a bit thinner, avoid fancy fabrics of any kind, which can give off the impression of an outfit without much definition. **Solid color clothing** made with supportive and well-shaped fabrics **help you take advantage of your curves rather than hiding them**.

Examples of garments that, thanks to a particular shape of the skirt (wide at the knee and tight at the waist), have a slimming effect

TO APPEAR A BIT TALLER

✓ If your legs aren't as long as you like, you can choose certain types of clothes that **make the waistline seem higher than your actual waistline**. You can get this result in one of two ways: either with high-waisted clothes or with sweaters that finish off lengthwise just below the glutes, covering where the upper leg meets the butt. The high-waisted approach applies to shirts and sweaters with a seam just below the breast. The long sweater approach can also work for jackets, shirts, and heavier winter jackets. The eye perceives the clothes much more, in fact, than your actual figure, and so by playing with hems and seams, you can render all imperfections invisible.

✓ Another trick to make your legs seem a bit longer and slimmer is to **adjust the hem exactly at the knee** (with skirts and coats) **or at the ankle** (with jeans and pants): **the thinner part of your leg is in evidence, and this produces an overall slimming effect**. The result will obviously be even better when paired with heels.

By adjusting the hem of skirts and coats at the knee you can make your legs appear longer and thinner

✓ For the same reason, it's best to carefully avoid those tube skirts that extend all the way down to mid-calf, which are only permissible on women with extremely thin legs who want to make them seem fuller. Skirts like these give the impression that the width of the calf continues along the whole leg.

✓ If you want to thin out the legs without necessarily resorting to high heels, it's fundamental to **choose shoes with a color equal to that of your legs**, whether that be light beige or nude if you're not sporting a tan, brown or leather colored if you're a bit more bronzed, or whatever color fits for your skin tone. Give it a try: beige shoes with a medium heel worn without tights (or with very thin tights in a nude color) make your legs appear so much longer and more slender compared to shoes that have a higher heel but are the wrong color for your skin.

Strapless shoes in a color that matches your skin slim the figure, even with a medium heel

- ✓ **The height of the waistline can also have an overall trimming effect**. Low-rise pants, which have been so trendy for years, don't slim anything, and wearing them requires a virtually perfect waistline because they're unforgiving. Instead, high-waisted pants have a natural slimming effect. In order to attain a kind of form-maintaining effect, it's vital to pick out the ones with stretch fabric, which beyond being more comfortable allows you to also have a kind of "sheath" effect, slimming out the waistline.

- ✓ If you are very young, by which I mean under thirty, another trick to flesh out a few inches in the legs is to **wear very short skirts**, adjusting the hem at around mid-thigh or even higher. In contrast, **miniskirts that come to just above the knee always make legs seem more robust and a bit shorter**.

- ✓ For those who feel a little short, but also for those who feel they have a few more pounds than they'd like and want to appear a bit slimmer, **boot-cut pants** (tight around the leg and knee but looser at the bottom) are a must wear, along with **high heels that are hidden under the pants**, lengthening your figure and visually cutting off a few pounds. You've got to try it to believe it! The boot-cut style is also perfect for those who have a strong calf, blending it in completely and making the legs come off as long and slender.

- ✓ Conversely, pants with a **large pant leg** worn by someone with a not exactly tall body wind up only **shortening your figure, even when combined with high heels**. Unfortunately, only the very tall women among us can sport these.

- ✓ At all costs, all women must absolutely **avoid baggy and high-hemmed pants** (a pattern that today is totally fashionable). They cut your figure shorter than it is and make even models' legs look stubby, so let's not even begin to think about what they do to those of us with "normal" legs! Look, there are things that should never be worn, and short baggy pants are a prime example.

FOR THOSE WHO'D LIKE TO HAVE MORE CURVES

- ✓ For those who aren't blessed with a big bust, the **use of pleats** in just the right places can work miracles because they provide volume to all the desired places. A **horizontal neckline can also help**, adding at least a half-measure, as shown in the image.

A horizontal neckline helps make the bust seem fuller, offering at least a half-measure more

- ✓ If you're feeling too thin, remember that **corduroy fabrics can effectively round out your form** and shape, making both seem fuller, so they are pitch perfect for those who'd like more prodigious curves.

- ✓ Also, for those who think they're too thin and would like to see themselves with a few more pounds, another suggestion is to wear **short jackets** that visually divvy up your figure in two and make you seem more full-figured.

- ✓ Simply wearing shoes of a color that contrasts with the complexion of your legs can help create a softer figure and provide you with a few curves; shoes with ankle straps work even better, as you can saw on the image from a few pages before.

Sticking with the theme of proportions, remember that, contrary to what you might think, **the height of the heel has to be *proportionate* to the length of the leg**.

And so, platform shoes and wildly crazy high heels are reserved, in an act of extreme injustice, for only those women with legs that go on for miles, especially if it's a closed shoe and not a sandal. On anything less than a statuesque body, from behind the heel would turn out looking longer than the calf, an unpleasant effect that would make the legs seem even shorter.

The only exception to this rule might be summer sandals with cork wedges, both because they're wonderfully informal and without any pretense to elegance and because sandals, leaving the foot partially uncovered, appear to lower the shoe, reducing in part the disproportionate effect that a high heel can often give.

And don't forget that even **accessories can be useful in playing around with proportions**.

For the short-statured ladies out there, the use of oversized bags is almost always an unwise choice given that huge bags tend to diminish the size of the person lugging them around. Along those lines, a teeny tiny bag snatched up by a tall woman or full-figured woman seems a bit out of place.

A handy tip to take to heart is that in order to see firsthand how a few minor tweaks can allow you to obtain the desired figure, you could ***try on your own to make some alterations to clothes you already have***, inspiring yourself by what we've covered so far and some images from this book or from a catalogue.

There's no need to be an expert: the vast majority of these changes can be made on the inside part of the clothing by inserting pleats and folds at strategic points, meaning that they can be done with seams that will remain unnoticed as they stay *inside* the clothes, and so their perfection is of zero importance!

Just arm yourself with a needle and thread and then give it a shot!

You may end up with some really terrific results at zero cost.

By doing this, you'll be able to adapt and personalize all the suggestions we've covered in these pages, experimenting with what best showcases your physique and **giving brand new life to clothes that are already in your closet**, all while discovering your very own style. There's no doubt, for instance, that the Artistic Woman, just as an example, doesn't give a damn about all the rules of symmetry and proportion, but this will never impede her from having an absolutely wonderful style all the same.

Above all, remember that in most cases **both our gifts and our imperfections help us equally** in following the path to find the style custom-made just for us, the one that allows us to find the inspiration to feel beautiful and fascinating in every moment.

XIV. Fabrics and Materials: The Importance of Yarn from Linen to Wool

The difference between style and fashion is quality.
—Giorgio Armani

A key element in the definition of our style is undoubtedly the **cloths and fabrics** with which our favorite and best clothes are made.

In the past, a lot of attention was paid to the choice of the textile with which a fabric was made. In fact, it represented one of the most fundamental aspects of clothing, in part because **it signaled out the differences between the wealthiest classes**—who could afford soft, precious, and refined fabrics—**and the poor classes**, who instead were expected to settle for much simpler fabrics (both in terms of processing and color), which were always much less comfortable to wear.

With the industrialization of production processes and the diffusion of ready-to-wear clothes, the quality of fabrics and textiles has seen a considerable decline and has become an almost secondary aspect to consider.

After several years of decline, however, the issue of fabric quality has come back into fashion and has even begun to be considered an essential element for ready-to-wear items, reversing the trend of using generically similar fabrics with mixed fibers and uniform appearance.

What this allows us, then, is an **extra tool with which we can personalize our style** and make sure that it's different from all the others, tweaking our outfits according the ever-changing times.

It's also interesting to remember that, historically speaking, textiles have always represented an important chapter in the European tradition of artisanal craftsmanship.

The importance of textiles as a commercial product began during the period of the Silk Trade with China, expanding later during the Renaissance with an unstoppable rise in Italian textile workshops, whose products were some of the most requested of the international market for luxury goods, thanks to their extraordinary beauty, their richness, and the technical perfection of velvet, damasks, and other fabrics.

Later, in nineteenth century Great Britain, the machines aiding in the industrial production of fabrics made their first appearance and eventually spread throughout the rest of the world.

Long ago, some textile processes were actually small artisanal masterpieces, and for that reason they were the exclusive **privilege of the rich people who displayed them in order to demonstrate their wealth and prestige**.

Today, even though it may be less easy to find fine fabrics, textiles are still one of the most important aspects of enriching our look in a unique and personalized way.

Experimenting with different fabrics and textiles allows us, among other things, to **emphasize the best characteristics of the style we've chosen**. It also adds a different tone to that selfsame color, all while multiplying the possible combinations to infinity.

Conversely, clothes made from uniform or standardized fabrics are in many cases done with cuts and colors exclusively for the current trend of the season, and this is why manufacturers don't care about investing in high-quality fabrics for such items.

Textiles differ both in terms of the **material** they're made of as well as the type of **processing** used in production. Cotton, for example, can be used both for pique fabrics (like the classic polo shirt) and for the denim that goes into jeans.

*The use of striking or distinguished fabrics
can make even simply cut clothes seem classy and refined*

At the same time, silk can be used to make satin (although these days it's frequently made with synthetics) and also chiffon, which is typically used for scarves, stoles, and pashminas both light and heavy.

The variation in fabrics is in fact practically limitless, representing a combination of material, processing, and sometimes even color, in the case of tartan (plaid), for example.

Below are some general suggestions you can dive into to enjoy yourself. And don't forget that if you wish to enrich your wardrobe with particular and unique items, you can easily **unearth special fabrics and threads at the market or in your parents' trunks in the attic**!

- ✓ Clothes made with cotton are fresh and practical, and they can easily become elegant simply by using some snazzy accessories. For a better range of wearability, cotton can be combined, in its composition, with a tiny percentage of synthetic material that will allow for a product where the quality of the raw material is matched with a perfect fit (but only as long as the percentage of synthetics is minimal).

- ✓ The use of fabrics in which the design is brought about not by printing but by using different-colored threads can make even a simple cloth garment interesting. It can also then be rendered even more sophisticated thanks to some details in a different fabric.

- ✓ The use of silks can provide clothes with an exceptional luminosity whose elegance gives them a fluid and easy-to-wear fit for all types of women.

- ✓ The use of lightweight fabrics with a splendid weave can allow you to make even simple cuts look terrific, resulting in an elegant and exclusive effect.

- ✓ Even the classic plaid (tartan), once considered staid and uninteresting by virtue of its origins, offers a number of varied uses and can be used even with extremely trendy patterns, giving you a look that's refined and informal at the same time.

In the appendix, you'll find a small technical guide that lists the most commonly used textiles and the most diffuse processes, along with the stories of each...with some curiosities thrown in that not everyone knows.

This may help you discover what their characteristics are and when they can be most useful, and it could be another way to discover something new so that you can **have a bit of fun with what you can potentially do with them**.

Besides, you might find a lot of pleasure in deepening your understanding of what suits you best and updating your style with the newest ideas and innovations.

Fabrics with a unique texture or details lend a fineness and character to the garments, turning them into polished items

But I have just one bit of advice: if you really want to know and appreciate the differences between all the materials and processes, **take a look at your mother's closet** or your aunts', trying to find in the attic or in one the hidden cabinets clothes from at least thirty to forty years ago, or even more if you're fortunate enough to find them.

In these old classics, you'll find **fabrics that are simply masterpieces**, and even if the patterns are not the most suited to you, you can still enjoy them by turning them into scarves, bags, belts, or skirts.

The result will be incredibly chic and absolutely unique.

XV. The Secrets of Versatility: Accessories (Without Exaggeration!)

> *Detail is as important as the essential.*
> *When it's inadequate, the whole outfit is ruined.*
> —Christian Dior

If colors represent the most visible aspect of our look, then accessories have a role that at first glance is more discrete but of no less importance.

We could even dare to say that accessories play—perhaps even in an unconscious way—the main role in **spelling out our character and our style**.

Here's a quick example to bring home this idea: imagine two friends dressed exactly the same way, in more or less neutral colors, with a pair of jeans or dark pants and a black or white sweater. Elsa decides to complete the outfit with a silk scarf, dark pumps with a medium heel, and a black leather bag. Stella chooses instead a multicolor scarf with fringe, low suede shoes, and a big loose woven bag.

The result is obvious. Just by adding accessories, we have a perfect example of the Classic Woman in the first case and the Informal Woman in the second. And despite the fact that they're both wearing identical basic garments, at first glance Elsa and Stella don't even seem comparably dressed because **the choice of different accessories has rendered them totally diverse**.

Accessories, then, don't merely represent a way to intensify our style or reinforce it. When the mood strikes, they also provide a way of utterly altering it, appearing—maybe only for just one day—completely different from usual, all without changing our base outfits.

It's worth remembering that with accessories—more than with any other aspect—**there's a risk of overdoing it**. After all, even if we wanted to, we couldn't wear more than one skirt or shirt at a time (although it's possible to see some fancy combinations like shorts with leggings). But with accessories, it's profoundly difficult to limit ourselves, because the choices available among scarves, pashminas, necklaces, bags, belts, and hats are so vast that it makes it so much less simple to make that decision.

So let's take a look at some ideas that can help **enrich our style in a personalized way without running the risk of going overboard**.

*Carefully selected accessories can make outfits pop
and complete the entire look, making everything more sophisticated*

An absolutely foolproof trick is giving preference to the things that seem striking to you—all the better if these things are made or reinvented by you.

One way to attain an unusual look is by playing around with accessories, giving them **a different function** than what they were originally intended to do. A light scarf, for example, can become a lovely belt, but also—if appropriately knotted—a super and surprising shopping bag.

In the same way, a large winter scarf made with lighter fabric can be used as luxurious shawl over a low-cut top or a light dress on cool summer evenings.

And what could be more original than **jewelry**, like necklaces or bracelets or even key chains, that are **put together with your own hands**? Among other things, these have the double advantage of being unique *and* being able to perfectly match everything that we have in our closets, because we can create them with the colors and materials most appropriate for our style.

Another idea I'm really crazy about is using scraps of high-quality furnishing fabrics,[1] which often have wonderful designs and patterns with well-paired colors, to put together absolutely inimitable scarves, unique belts, or unmatched bags.

As for basic accessories, like shoes and handbags, here are some guidelines to help make the process easier:

✓ **Bags and shoes don't necessarily need to be the same color** (especially when it comes to more out-there colors). A red bag, for example, is generally most graceful when worn with shoes in a standard leather color. Wearing such a bag with a pair of red shoes could seem excessive or out-of-place for your outfit, in addition to seeming overly thought-out. (As we've seen, real elegance is always spontaneous.)

---

[1] You can easily find them in the textile sample books that furniture stores periodically renew. If you ask, when new arrivals come to the store the shopkeeper will be more than happy give you some old ones that you can go to town on to your heart's content.

- ✓ The choice of **shoe color**, as we've pointed out, is **fundamental if our goal is to appear a little bit thinner**, but it's also something that can bring about some doubts regarding the proper color combination with bags and other accessories. The simplest thing in this case is to **choose bags and accessories that have the same type of *tonality* (warm or cold)**.

- ✓ For example, if you choose beige shoes with slightly brown tones (warm tonality) you can combine them with leather colored accessories, but also ochre, brown, or other colors containing a warm hue. If you instead choose grayish footwear, leaning more toward a cooler shade, you can easily pair them with other cool tonalities like white, ice blue, charcoal, sand, or taupe. The result, in both cases, will be absolutely flawless.

On the other hand, throwing in **some accessories—even just one—with contrasting tones** and pairing it with a monochrome outfit with mostly subdued colors **can immediately brighten up the whole outfit**.

In this way, a super classic and nearly boring iron-gray or total-black pantsuit can get reborn, transforming into something vivacious and mischievous simply by adding an orange bag.

And the serene elegance of an entirely blue dress becomes a complete chic outfit just by adding a necklace with metal detailing and a handle bag with some metal details.

Beyond bags and shoes, most of us possess accessories with a more decorative rather than practical function. More than anything, these elements allow us to enrich our style, despite being superfluous from a strictly practical point of view. And even with that said, they still need to be carefully selected, remembering that the perfect accessory turns into **a detail that characterizes our look, oftentimes more often than our main clothes**. With minimal cost and effort, these well-chosen accessories allow us to immediately personalize our outfits with an emphasis on our style.

Accessories with contrasting colors can illuminate and diversify a monochromatic look

To make this choice easier, let's look at some suggestions:

- ✓ For accessories that rest **close to the face**, it's best to give preference to **shiny, reflective materials**: an iridescent scarf, for example, or a necklace made with big pieces of metal or glass. This will add some light to your face, guaranteeing it a lovely radiance even on a dark day full of nothing but rain.

- ✓ **Avoid objects claiming to be artisanal but which are clearly mass-produced**. Even the most elegant and cared-for outfits would lose all class with products like these.

✓ If you're late for an important appointment and haven't yet picked out your accessories, it's best to **take only the most indispensable ones**, like scarves and gloves (in winter months). A hasty choice of one single item can completely disrupt the desired effect of the outfit that you may have spent hours in front of the mirror studying.

In all cases, make sure to use just a few elements; your look should be minimal, and you must refrain from overflowing it with stuff, even if perhaps each and individual item seems valuable.[2]

Pay attention also to **socks and stockings**, which are currently all the rage in terms of colors and patterns.

---

[2] To give you a better idea of the effect that a look overloaded with accessories can give, I'll give you an example of a different kind but one that's equally illustrative. Think about shop windows; the most elegant ones always display just a few items with an air of great value, even if in reality they aren't. In contrast, when a shop window is overflowing with objects, you aren't able to make any one thing out from the other and even the valued items go unnoticed.

Since the use of bright colors and fanciful designs undeniably place a spotlight on the legs, only those with super thin legs should try these types of items, or those of us who have an infallible aesthetic taste, originating from a background and a preparation that cannot be improvised. **Pairing them in a flawless way with other garments requires experience and care**, and the risk of unpleasant slipups is higher with these items than with other accessories that can be matched in a less challenging way.

Here is one last note about **bags and shoes**.

They are, for sure, one of the most essential components of the look. Despite being defined as accessories, they have almost nothing to do with typical accessories. These are indispensable items, in the sense that these are things you truly cannot go without, while you can obviously do without a scarf or head out of the house without a hat.

Unlike other clothing, though, handbags and shoes possess an appeal that could be called **a magnetic and irresistible attraction**.

This is demonstrated by the fact that during an outing where we're trying to refrain from buying anything at all we're more or less able to resist the expanse of sweaters and jackets no matter how fashionable they are. But in front of a pair of shoes, we're practically defenseless.

The reasons for this attraction are various, and many of them are surely physiological, given that you see girls as early as one and half or two giddy with joy after the purchase of their desired little shoes.

On the one hand, feet are practically the only part of our body that we are able to see in full without resorting to the mirror, making them the sweetest, most satisfying purchase of all because **we can admire these objects of our desire even as we're wearing them**. The same also obviously is valid for bags, whereas this can't be said of skirts or sweaters, at least if you don't want to appear eccentric.

The other possible reason for their appeal is that **shoes** (as well as bags, obviously) **aren't affected by our fluctuations in weight**.

Even if you're coming off a major Christmas binge, *your shoe size remains always the same.*

Try all the shoes you want—they're *always* going to fit perfectly.

For this reason, and for many others, buying shoes and bags, for a woman, is *always* gratifying.

Husbands, partners, and fathers take note: *this is the way it is.*

We can't change what's written in our DNA, and you might as well accept it, since *there's nothing you can do about it.*

Apart from giving us another pair of sandals.

XVI. What Should I Wear Today? Character and Personality for Every Occasion

Someone once said that **true elegance consists of simply wearing the right clothes for the right occasion**.
Nothing could be more true.
Of course, the idea of the classic look that remains graceful regardless of place or occasion, doesn't actually exist. What *does* exist is a wide variety of ways to style yourself: while **still remaining bold and unique, you can effortlessly match your stylishness to what's around you**.
Just think about it: you go to a casual event like a big party in the countryside and you see someone dressed very formally, in a suit or an evening dress—a look that is typically considered universally "elegant." Given the context, you would never in a million years consider this person's outfit the height of elegance. At very best, if we're being polite, it would seem bizarre. The bluntest of us might say that it was just ridiculous.

It's just like the timeless Coco Chanel once said: "**Fashion is at once a caterpillar and a butterfly, caterpillar by day and butterfly by night**. We need dresses that crawl and dresses that fly. A butterfly does not go to a market, and a caterpillar does not go to a party."
Thus, choosing which clothes will be more suitable for each moment of our day takes on a fundamental importance in the definition of our style. Feeling comfortable doesn't only depend

on feeling at ease in what we're wearing but also on *how appropriate* it feels for the places we want to go to, the things we have to do, and the people we're going to meet. Two final things to keep in mind are climate and **weather conditions**; considering that the chicest pumps lose all their class if they've become a pool of water, it's better in those cases to pull out a nice pair of boots, undeniably the most resistant to pouring rain.

So **what's the secret to feeling perfectly at ease no matter the context or place**? The best way to find your inner fashion Zen fit for all circumstances is to simply **stick to your own style**.

The results will be even more amazing if you stick to **high-quality fabrics and accessories**—and remember, that *doesn't* necessarily mean branded!

Just as an example, a garment that is typically not considered the height of elegance, like a pair of **jeans**, can reveal itself to be **wonderful, even for formal situations, if it is made with high-quality fabrics** that never lose their shape and have an excellent fit. This is especially true **when the jeans are worn by the Informal Woman and paired with some striking accessories**.

The same is true in the opposite way for the **classic black sheath dress**, which is normally considered a safe bet for every type of formal context. **If chosen with a poor textile, the dress will lose all of its elegance** or wind up appearing completely out of place: if your style is more aligned with the Green Woman, who wouldn't ever feel comfortable dressed like this, you will give the impression of being awkward and lacking in *charme*.

The secret, then, lies in finding within each style the inspiring references that make up the individual variables in our choices and then playing around with them, giving more **emphasis to the main items that help us clearly identify our own style**.

In addition to having a positive effect on the budget, we can all also watch as our *charme* and spontaneity increase.

So let's take a peek together at the key moments of the day, discovering how **just by changing a few details, we can adapt our look for all occasions**.

AT WORK

Apart from a few exceptions, by now the majority of jobs and work environments operate with an expectation of **business casual attire**. Even when men are required to wear a jacket and a tie, there is usually immense freedom of choice in women's clothing.

Set free, then, all the clothes that you love the most, both informal, like jeans (not torn!) and sweaters, and formal, like pantsuits and blouses.

There's only one caution: **avoid excessively show-offy outfits and items**, and instead show a preference for serious cuts and lines. Or in any case, limit any potential garments of a more particular variety to only a few details.

For a day at the office, choose both classic-cut garments and more casual and informal outfits

In other words, even if you've just brought home a beautiful embroidered sweater and you can't wait to show it off, save it for a night out on the town.

In contrast, a really unique light scarf can be worn casually as long as you have the foresight to combine it with an outfit that's otherwise soberly styled.

Shoes can be either low- or high-heeled, but be sure to **avoid both overly sporty models and extremely elegant ones** made with materials better prepared for a night out, like silver, gold, or rhinestones, for example.

EATING OUT

Deciding on an outfit for a dinner obviously **depends on the specifics of the place where the dinner will be held**.

If the restaurant is a formal place, a simple sheath dress with a jacket should be just fine with elegant shoes and a lovely bag for those who lean toward more formal pieces of clothing (like the Classic Woman, the Sophisticated Woman, and the Sexy Woman) or a pair of pants with a stylish top and an eye-catching jacket for those with a more informal nature (the Artistic, Sporty, Green, Trendy, and Informal Woman).

On the other hand, if the restaurant is more of a country-style mom-and-pop kind of place, here an elegant number will have you looking way out of place. A restaurant like this would be just the right fit for low-heeled boots and shoes with casual, unshowy clothes.

If you don't know the location and are doubting your choices, you can opt for a highly versatile outfit put together with a **neutral base, which may consist of pants with a well-fitted but simply cut top**. Pair these with a jacket or a bag, all made from **high-quality fabrics or unusual materials**. This is a foolproof solution that can be worn at every age and by every type of figure, one that **lends itself readily to every environment**.

Neutral garments made from striking fabrics can provide for a foolproof outfit appropriate for many occasions

If you prefer to wear **skirts** instead, keep in mind that for formal events they generally work most flawlessly for all styles and body types when they're **knee-length**, which turns out to look pleasantly sophisticated while being neither too conspicuous nor too serious.

If you're heading out for something more informal, both miniskirts and maxiskirts can be terrific options.

Calf-length skin-hugging skirts, however, are usually unsuitable. They are a bit too serious, and besides skirts of this length and pattern have an undoubtedly frustrating effect on the leg line.

For formal environments, the knee-length skirt gives off a pleasantly elegant look without seeming too serious

If you like wearing a **jacket**, consider that in general it's much **easier to match it with a dress**, while matching it with a skirt can be more difficult: whichever style you choose, it will result in a wonderfully feminine and elegant outfit, neither too flashy nor too self-serious.

IN YOUR FREE TIME

The clothes you wear during your free time have to be **comfortable without giving up your overall style**. Also during these times, a big help comes from a **careful use of accessories** (bags and scarves in particular), which allows us to **make our look seem immediately polished and elegant despite being built from comfortably informal base-level garments** like sweaters, pants, or overcoats.

For a night out in the city or an afternoon spent shopping, light coats and short jackets are just about perfect, with heaviness and fabrics varying depending on the season. Clothes like this, which each one of us will pick out in our own way, have the advantage of being easily matched with pants, skirts, and dresses alike. They also allow our look to be adaptable to sudden changes in weather without having to stuff our bags full of sweaters.

If you're heading out of the city, **jeans** (or **corduroys**, for the most traditional women out there) are indispensable. In the hottest months, they can be switched out and replaced with **shorts of all lengths and type**, combined with a sports jacket or a top—a polo shirt for those who slant traditionalist or a vividly designed blouse for those with more of a creative streak.

The use of unusual fabrics or accessories can be a useful way of being stylish without sacrificing comfy clothes

There's another point that may seem too obvious but in reality, for those die-hard high-heelers out there, is not obvious at all: if you're headed for a country destination or even if you are taking a quick trip that might involve some uneven earthy surfaces, leave the heels at home and forget about the skin-hugging tube skirts.

"But," I can already hear you saying, "I always want to feel elegant. How can I feel chic wearing horrendous hiking boots?"

If this is your objection, be aware that **thin heels and tight skirts**, though they may be elegant in the city, **are anything but stylish when shown off in rural settings**, not to mention on the rougher hiking terrains.

Jeans combined with vivid tops or a dress made in a soft fabric make for a practically stylish outfit

True elegance, as we've pointed out, consists of wearing the right and suitable clothes for the given situation, and there's nothing less appropriate on a hiking trail in the mountains than high heels and tight skirts.

If you're reluctant to give up that touch of femininity, reach for sandals tied at the ankle with a small wedge paired with knee-pants or Capri pants, or even a pleated skirt with flat shoes.

Another really practical choice and pleasant outfit is based on leggings worn with a large, long pullover and some ballerina flats, which offer a touch of class while remaining absolutely practical.

A simple dress with a straight cut featuring some interesting finishing details can also be perfect for trips outside the city that may include stops at museums or an art show, since simple outfits like this combine practicality with classic and elegant models in an easygoing way.

In this way, **both your femininity and your class remain intact**.

And your feet will no doubt be grateful.

XVII. Let's Party! Charming Outfits for Special Occasions

So-called special occasions are inevitably the biggest causes of what we could safely define as Empty Closet Syndrome for most of us, that moment when upon opening up our closet, filled with clothes of all varieties, we find ourselves exclaiming in a raised voice: "But I have nothing to wear!"

This scene, incidentally, which film and television reproduce continuously, usually only triggers a big laugh in the male audience; for us women, because we've gone through this experience with all its pathos many times, it is anything but a laughing matter.

And what's more, looking at photos of weddings, graduations, and parties of any kind, you realize that the attempt to dress *stylishly* can really produce some results that are quite different from what was intended.

Let me share an instructive anecdote. Not so long ago, I happened to be passing in front of a university right as a recent graduate waltzed out the university's doors with all those crowned laurels on her head, surrounded by a small crowd of celebrating friends and family.

Poor thing that she was, in addition to being all made up and coiffed like a variety show actress (obviously ill-advised by her mother, who was sporting the same look), she was just *so* incredibly overdressed, wearing a short lace dress with a velvet handbag covered in rhinestones and platform shoes with a nearly five-centimeter sole and a heel of at least fourteen centimeters. Clearly not used to wearing such outrageous heels, this unfortunate thing, after just a few steps on the pavement, tripped and fell to the ground in the middle of all the clamor. Struggling to her feet after the nasty fall, the just-minted graduate shrugged the dust off and continued marching with a slight limp, held up and carried along by her mother. Rather than well on her way to a bright future, she looked like someone on her way home after night of heavy boozing.

Now, if we allow that it's true that not all choices for special occasions end up having such a hilarious result, it's also true that in any case **the desire to wear something different from the usual in hopes of appearing more elegant can easily sweep us quite far away from our own style**, leading us to make choices that don't work on us at all.

All this ends up doing is making us absurdly a whole lot less elegant than what we normally wear on our day-to-day outings.

So let's take a look at some examples that combine simplicity and style so that we can look our absolute best even in our most significant moments.

DURING THE DAY

Nowadays, many important events take place during the day, which to some extent makes the choice a bit easier since even some informal numbers are easily adaptable to more formal situations with just a few tricks.

The main types of outfits perfect for these types of occasions are divided into **two categories: the traditionalist and the nonconformist**.

In the first case (traditionalists), the universally accepted choice is a suit or, even better, **a dress with a matching color**

jacket. The dress option is a bit easier and produces a better finish than, say, a skirt and a shirt combo, and the reason for this is obvious: finding the right combination is so much easier.

The more clothes we wear, the more difficult pairing them together becomes.

Conversely, if you're not wearing so many different garments, like a dress and a jacket in this case, the choice gets streamlined and what you end up with is typically so much more wonderful.

A knee-length dress made from fine fabric remains a well-established choice for more formal occasions

Let's try an example. A dress in patterned fabric can be combined with a jacket in any one of the colors present in the dress' design, and it'll easily be a sophisticated and chic outfit. On the other hand, a patterned skirt has to be matched both with the top and the jacket, making the decisions less easy and not nearly as immediate.

And we can't overlook the fact that **dresses are naturally figure-slimming items**, while skirts, if they're not carefully selected, can often make the person wearing them seem a bit bigger.

Continuing with the traditionalists, another factor not to be undervalued pertains to the choice of the color of the outfit. If we opt for a solid color, we should then choose from tones most suitable for us: it's always best to **avoid choosing colors that seem too different from our usual choices** that would in all likelihood leave us feeling ill at ease. When choosing patterned designs, the choices available are much more vast and they even allow us to dare for some unusual colors resulting in something extremely pleasant.

As for the nonconformists, the choice becomes greater, in the sense that you can easily obtain a satisfying result simply by **adding one or two more elegant items to a set of clothes more or less in line with your traditionally nontraditional daily outfit**.

For example, a jacket or a coat made with a striking fabric, as well as a bag and shoes with an out-of-the-ordinary cut and color, can all help put together an elegant look while still remaining casual and spontaneous.

Also, keep in mind **that the characteristics of the event are what guide us in choosing what to wear, especially for colors**. So, for example, outfits with more formal and subdued colors (like night blue, black, and gray, brown remaining a bit inelegant) go perfectly for work lunches or graduate thesis discussions, all of which are connected in some way to a working environment, while pastel outfits are more suitable for ceremonies like weddings, engagement parties, and similar events.

Gray, black, and other subdued colors are most applicable to formal situations, like meetings or graduations or work lunches

Similarly, a gray pantsuit, no matter how beautiful or well-tailored it is, will end up looking very out of place at a dance party.

As for **shoes**, if you usually wear heels no higher than three to four centimeters, don't risk your ankles for your sister-in-law's wedding; instead, **go for some high-quality shoes in a color that particularly speaks to you**. You can even venture to try a bright color, since shoes are nowhere near the face, but always be sure to **keep them to a fit and a heel analogous to what you normally wear**. Your overall look will benefit from this, and at the reception you'll able to head for the dance floor rather than sitting it all out because your feet hurt.

A pastel-colored outfit is always delightful for weddings and parties, while remaining ill-suited for work-related events

AT NIGHT

There are two primary factors in deciding on a nighttime outfit that isn't for a fancy dinner. On the one hand, the choice can seem more difficult with respect to the quotidian outfits, while on the other hand, it's also true that it's a chance to **have a bit of fun with more unusual choices** that you've always wanted to play around with but never found the right occasion for.

For those who lean a bit more on the classic side, rooted in tradition, the suggestion is to opt for some pretty straightforward solutions, **experimenting perhaps with the preciousness and the sheen of the fabric in both the main garment and the accessories** (using silk and chiffon, for example, but also lace, velvet, and satin), always avoiding out-of-the-ordinary cuts and colors.

A simple silk dress (in the hot seasons) or velvet (in the cold ones) provides an elegant look and always ends up being perfect for the more traditionalist styles

For those who have fun experimenting with new, surprising combinations, these types of social events can provide an opportunity to throw on a multicolored dress or go all out with daring hairstyles and makeup.

Now for those who don't stick their noses up at more outré clothes, if the occasion calls for it, then **a dress with an asymmetrical bottom (something which also trims the figure)** can be a really captivating choice.

Here, the choice of fabrics and "precious" accessories remains as crucial as ever. Be sure to **avoid the use of low-quality fabrics** at all costs when trying to come up with an elegant outfit.

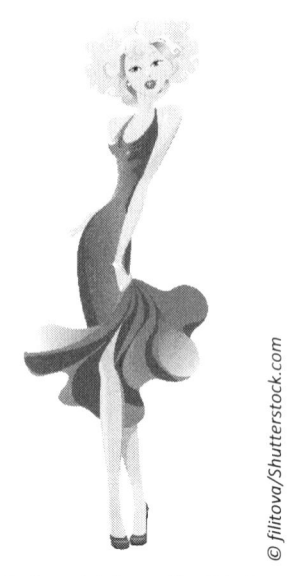

Asymmetrical dresses made from high-quality fabrics aren't as demanding as long dresses and are much easier in general in terms of wearability

If you have an even more whimsical character, feel free to fully indulge in imaginative and lavish creations without imposing any limitations on the choice of fabrics, colors, or accessories.

Everyone will definitely remember you by the end of the night, but after all, isn't that what you want?

XVIII. The Closet: How to Organize It Perfectly in Three Steps

One of the ways to be sure that you will always be ready quickly, simply, and pleasantly is by maintaining a perfectly organized closet. In this way, you'll quickly be able to find what you're looking for, avoiding that hunt for your favorite scarf just a minute before going out for a really important appointment.

If you always keep a careful watch on all your clothes and **avoid simply wearing four or five items and ignoring another seventy**, you'll be able to **try some unusual combinations** that are different from what you might normally choose and could be really quite surprising.

To give you some guidance, I'll take a few cues from my book *La Casa di Charme*, in which, among other things, I discuss the subject of wardrobe management with the objective of improving the systemization of our closets, making our daily ritual of choosing an outfit easier and quicker, while at the same time **carving our closet into a pleasant space that's both practical and well-organized**.

There are three basic steps you can take to optimize the management of your wardrobe: choosing the clothes, creating more space, and establishing a new sense of order.

Let's look in detail at what all this really means and how we can do it in the best way possible.

CHOOSING THE CLOTHES

When reorganizing your closet, the first thing to take care of above all is sorting out all your clothes in order to highlight the least used garments:
- ✓ the clothes that have grown stale
- ✓ the clothes that, although lovely, don't go so well with any of the other items you have
- ✓ those other items that, while they may be pleasing, may have fallen out of style due to their color or because the pattern appears outdated

The ideal thing would be to pick out 30 to 40 percent of the clothes like this, **keeping those that match each other together in one place while "archiving" the others**.

Having made that choice, which it's better to do on a day when you have a good chunk of free time, you'll immediately realize how taking care of your closet can be both easy and fun.

You'll be able to find clothes that are already ready to go, which you'll be able to easily match without getting confused by all the other huge quantities of stuff in the closet that only clutters the space and that you so rarely use.

But please take my advice and **store some of those eliminated clothes—if they're well-made with fine fabrics—** above the closet instead of throwing them away. **If they are high-quality items, they will probably reveal themselves as once again highly wearable within a few years**, taking the place of those that in the meantime have lost their allure or that you don't like anymore. You will then realize how clothes that you've gotten tired of can magically come back to delight you, while those that once stubbornly refused to match with what you had will suddenly lend themselves to a new bag or jacket. **You'll rediscover these things with joy as though they were new**.

For clothes that are made of fabric of poor quality or that have become ruined or lost their color, it's another story completely. If dyeing (see chapter XX in the third part of this book) appears impractical or if the fabric, over time and after laundry cycles, has proven to be of minimal quality, then it's for the best to get rid of the garments altogether, because most likely you'll never end up wearing them again.

If, instead, you have a garment constructed from a pattern that is particularly striking on you, you can put it to the side (but don't forget to keep it in a distinct place, away from the everyday clothes) to help you find another one like it. Or you can even try to make a similar one of your own. Why not?

MAKING MORE SPACE

The second thing to do when it comes to wardrobe management and making the outfit selection process quick and easy—not to mention successful—is to figure out how to **amplify the space available**, maximizing the use of the spaces provided and the perception of the clothes on display.

In this way, we can avoid the problem of certain garments being relegated to the bottom of the drawer only to wind up being forgotten, even though they might be just the thing we're looking for on a special evening, not to mention those nights when we're complaining about how we have nothing to wear.[3]

The ideal method for creating some parity between practicality and visibility would be **adding some drawers where everything we have is on full display**. In this regard, trying to integrate drawers with shelves can be a useful trick; **the clothes should preferably be arranged by color tone** (light, dark, or bright) or even by type (high neck or V-neck, for example, or long-sleeved and short-sleeved).

Sorting by color is always preferable, because items organized by color are so nice to see, so you could simply add **some shelves**

---

[3] Phrases uttered with at least bi-weekly frequency by practically every woman on the planet. Even if in our heart we're well aware that it's a bald-faced lie, partners and husbands might fall for it and thereby pardon us for the purchase of yet another pair of shoes.

in your bedroom where you could put those items; this will help you increase the available space, and putting in new shelves is surely easier than buying a new closet!

As for the interior of the closet, believe it or not, there is often some unused space that you can take advantage of, and a few tips should suffice.

First of all, it's a good idea to rethink the interiors of our closets by adding extra shelves and boxes or other containers. For example, shelves can usually be easily moved higher or lower simply by moving the appropriate holders, and it's preferable to adjust them so that every inch of height in the closet is taken advantage of.

Above all, **add as many shelves as possible** to avoid having massive piles of shirts and sweaters that become impossible to manage.[4]

Another way to make the most of the space you have is to measure the maximum height of your jackets and dresses on their hangers and use these dimensions as the height of the principal compartment of the closet in such a way that allows more space to be opened up for the upper shelves.

For the top shelves, if you're usually inclined to put boxes containing off-season clothes up there, then it's wise to move the shelves so that they are situated to fit *exactly* two boxes, one on top of the other. Although a few centimeters might not seem so decisive, try it out for yourself. You'll be amazed by how much space you can create in the end.

For small pieces of clothing (daytime underwear, for example, or socks) **small drawers are your best bet**; the size of a bedside table cabinet, for example, is perfect for these items.[5] The fact that they are located outside of the closet instead of

---

[4]Additional shelves to be inserted inside cupboards or cabinets can usually be found commercially prepared and at reasonable prices.

[5]To make better use of the drawer space, you can divide them into many different compartments. The easiest and cheapest way is to use old shoe boxes so that when you do the seasonal restock, they can simply be stored with all their contents on the highest shelves without having to empty them.

inside is a negligible detail given that these are typically stand-alone clothes, meaning that they don't have to match your outfits (this also allow you to use small drawers that can be put everywhere to store some extra stuff).

Larger drawers can instead be used for shirts and sweaters. Another suggestion is **creating a two-layered drawer**: below, a box for the less frequently used items like a red holiday outfit or an old nightgown you still have affection for, and above, the more everyday articles.

As for the interior fittings of the closet, beyond shelves and crates it's fundamental to have **one or two mirrors on the inside-facing side of the door**, or even better—if you have the option—choose closets already fitted with mirrored doors. Beyond making the room look bigger, these allow you to immediately study what effect a sweater with a pair of pants will have and also the effect of your overall appearance at that moment.

The spaces of our closets can be supported, if necessary, by shelves and sections placed in a hidden position (behind the door, for example) or even in the storage closet. A small shelving unit with shelves even just twenty centimeters in depth, for example, will allow you to lay out all your bags and maybe even a few pairs of shoes.

And then if you go all out and decide to **display your stylish and fanciful bags and shoes,** the shelves can also be positioned **in plain sight rather** than tucked away behind the door, which is both original as well as a cute way of checking it all out.

ESTABLISHING A NEW ORDER

The importance of the order and the subdivision of clothes and accessories among all the dressers, closets, and shelves, cannot be neglected; when all the spaces are "ordered" as they should be, the selection process will be undeniably easier.

However, the word *order* here has a different meaning than it usually does; the object isn't to urge you to get your closet and all your clothes and accessories *in order* but rather to do the opposite and *change their place*.

When this is done, it'll be **so much easier to find them again as well as put them away**. But how do we decide what is the most perfect location for each item?

The answer is easy: it's the *first place* you've looked for it during those moments when you weren't able to find it anywhere.

To manage your closet with more ease, then, you must *change* the place of the clothes that normally seem to evade you and *replace them* in the locations where you instinctively try to find them when they're missing.

You've lost hours looking for that favorite shawl or that evening clutch that you don't often use, haven't you? Well, as soon as you are able to find what you're looking for—after extensive research and after arguing with your sister and accusing her of taking your things without asking—the wiser thing is to go ahead and **put that item right back in the first place you tried to find it** and *keep it there*, because that's exactly where you'll go hunting for it the next time…and next time you'll find it in no time at all.

PART THREE

Timeless Charme

XIX. *Charme* and Style at Any Age

Elegance is the only beauty that never fades.
—Audrey Hepburn

As far back as ancient times, women have always had an innate passion for their *look*, meaning not only the clothes they wear but also their accessories, makeup, hair, and so on.

Despite this natural predisposition, however, the look a woman sets out with in reality often turns out quite different from what she was hoping for.

Part of this is because the time we can dedicate to ourselves is always not nearly enough, and part is because the clothes we like always seem to be crazily expensive. But above all—let's just admit it—it's also because sometimes laziness gets the best of us. Also, we convince ourselves that as long as we fail to lose those five pounds or find the time to go the hairstylist, our appearance is less than satisfying, so it's not even worth losing any time over.

Dear friends, let me say that if you have found yourselves thinking these thoughts, you couldn't be more mistaken—**every woman has the ability to feel comfortable and polished**, and all with very little effort. And most of all, contrary to what you might think, **this is just as true for those of us who have already watched thirty-five years pass**.

Yes, you read that right. Having a neat, smart appearance that satisfies us can paradoxically be easier at the age of fifty than at twenty.

Of course, I'm not specifically speaking about smooth skin or tiny hips (although these days there are women in their fifties and up with more knockout legs than those in their twenties; they just might not be showing them off).

Instead, I'm talking about **a pleasant and well-cared-for appearance**, an attractive look that transmits energy and positivity. However hard it is to believe, it's easier to reach this look with the passing of the years for the simple reason that **with time, the greater understanding of ourselves, and the refinement of our tastes, it gets easier to obtain what we desire** because we understand ourselves so much better now.

Having a personalized and impressive look—maybe even a bit eccentric, but never trashy—at twenty isn't easy.

There are certainly women in their twenties who can pull it off, but those women are endowed with an exceptional gift for aesthetic appeal and an uncommonly found sense of inbuilt good taste.

There are also young women who, stimulated by a personal inclination or desire to work in fashion or in an artistic field, devote themselves to this with consistency and regularity, reading books, magazines, and blogs, and they're able to build this kind of capacity that's not so common among their contemporaries.

Speaking generally, though, **understanding how to seize our best qualities** and discovering what works on us and makes us sparkle the most **takes years**. The same amount of years is also required to be able to decide which outfit is the most suitable for us and for the occasion at hand and to be able draw out with certainty which makeup suits our style most. To say the least, these strokes of aesthetic wisdom, all of them, require experience and practice.

Specifically for this reason, it's often easier to achieve our desired look when we're a little older, which is to say when we're able to expertly pick out what brings out our beauty, leaving us feeling charming and comfortable with ourselves and with others in a way that remains impervious to time's caprices.

The secret to self-care and taking stock of ourselves lies in tapping into who we really are and showing that to the world, **highlighting all our strengths and amplifying them**.

Figuring this out, unless you have an infallible sense of these kinds of things, requires practice, patience, and time.

*An elegant and classy look is easier to achieve
when you can identify what makes you sparkle the most
and when the style most custom-fitted to you has been underlined*

When a young woman in the eighteen to twenties range sets out to choose her outfit for a party—assuming she isn't blessed with a particular sixth sense for good taste—she focuses on the clothes, the shoes, and the accessories rather than on her own physique or face.

She considers the color and the cut exclusively according to the brand, assessing whether it's still in fashion or already out-of-date, and she does so mostly without paying much attention to how she actually *looks*.

She may choose flashy makeup that fails to highlight her best features but weighs them down instead. Or she may use no makeup at all.

All of this can usually be justified at a young age—but not always, given that most young women have forms vastly different from the pipette-thin silhouette of models as well as far from perfect skin. The result, often, is a look that risks being terribly unkempt, if not in bad taste.

Conversely, the more the years pass, the more we develop an awareness of, on the one hand, what suits us best and makes us look our best, and on the other hand, the importance of **finding an outfit that's not only aesthetically harmonious but also sets off our personality**. It's this aspect that truly allows us to feel most beautiful and fascinating, together with the capacity to pick out with the highest degree of certainty just what it is that's appropriate for us for a specific occasion.

The styles that we saw in the first part of the book start from the premise that giving preference to one style over another serves to point us toward a certain type of character. The mere fact that the same article of clothing that might look perfect on one woman with a specific type of personality but make another one feel awkward and clumsy illustrates this expertly.

And so our choices are never solely aesthetic, but rather they stem from our personality and our identity.

Jumping off from some common elements, every style reveals itself in millions of different ways that arise from the distinct character of each one of us and is filtered through **a reworking of elements, colors, and materials that merge together in perfect harmony**.

And for this reason, the more the years go by and the more we've refined our sense of self-awareness and our overall understanding of our own style, this coming together of all the ingredients gets so much easier to attain.

The rest just comes by itself.

Why, you may be asking?

Because once you've figured out what works for you, it ends up being incredibly easy to define it further from a practical point of view, first outlining the basic cuts and then enriching it with all those flourishes and details that really make everything pop, all while avoiding anything that muddles those ideas.

When our taste has been refined and our style is clearly outlined, it becomes so much easier to pick out the clothes, the hairstyle, and the makeup for a specific occasion, as well as being able to confidently grab the most suitably matching scarf, bag, and necklace.

Or another way it could play out is that, for example, you decide on a scarf that you're particularly dead-set on wearing and then you go on to craft your whole outfit around it. The results will be imaginative and surprising.

Returning to the initial theme, I remember I once ran into a friend of mine (in her thirties at the time) who was with her mother, who was in her sixties. They looked like twins in terms of their colors and features. Without a doubt my friend is cute, but what really hit me was the *charme* emanating from her mother. Her appearance and her manner just burst with energy, self-confidence, and positivity, all without the intervention of any kind of cosmetic surgery or artifice.

She wore light and well-applied makeup, groomed hair, classy clothes, and a contagious smile, all of which was so much more attractive than a look characterized only by high-fashion items or by surgically enhanced breasts flaunted in plain sight.

On this note I would like to add that, although I'm not personally opposed to **plastic surgery** in order to manage defects that we really just can't bear, I find it to be **absolutely counter-productive when it's used to try to make you appear always in your twenties at all costs**.

I'm sure you've had one of those experiences where you've come across a woman whose face was absolutely smooth but, inexplicably, who seemed so much older than the fascinating woman well beyond her forties at her side, just as we've all seen famous actresses lose all their *charme* and appeal after one too many cosmetic retouchings, and yet in all probability they were entrusted to the biggest names in the industry with no expenses spared.

The reason why these cosmetic surgeries promising a younger appearance often fail is that **once we're past thirty, our beauty is the sum of our features *and* our expression**.

For this reason, a girl who wasn't always the most immediately stunning teenager can, when she's older, turn into a truly beautiful woman, all because her intelligent expression and self-confident countenance help to shape her features day-by-day, making them more captivating even when marked gently by age.

In the same way, a young girl with absolutely perfect features but a negative personality who isn't exactly the brainiest in her group already at forty years (if not a bit prior) is going to find herself with a face wearing the timeworn evidence of that disgruntled expression, losing every trace of beauty.[6]

For these reasons, the surgical procedures that attempt to cancel out the expression and render the face inexpressive rarely end in satisfaction because, after our twenties, **it's truly our expressivity that becomes a fundamental component of our beauty**. If we get rid of our expressions, our *charme* is reduced to nothing.

At a certain age, a woman has to choose between seeming young or being charming, because **the true challenge for a woman is to be beautiful while showing her age**.

From a practical perspective, there are undeniable advantages involved in this, among some other things; after all, continuing to look young requires not only a ton of money for the cosmetic surgeries (which can be annoying and not free from risks) but also a whole lot of time spent in the gym and having massages and treatments of all kinds.

On the other hand, to make you captivating and charming, you only need **your own good taste, a positive personality, and a certain amount of energy**—all things that, by the mere fact of being a woman, each one of us possesses in great quantity.

---

[6]Incidentally, the same is even true for men. No doubt you've had the occasion of running across, after twenty years, the guy who was once the most handsome in high school (and who wasn't necessarily brilliant intellectually) rendered so much less handsome by his not exactly clever expression.

XX. *Retro Charme*: Learning from the Past

Fashion always reflects the times in which we live, though when the times are trivial, we prefer to forget it.
—Coco Chanel

You've undoubtedly noticed that in recent years, an increasing resurgence of **patterns, cuts, and models from the past** has been catching fire, both thanks to the proliferation of vintage shops as well as thanks to the specific choices of various fashion *maisons*.

In particular **the period between the '40s and the '50s** is one that currently carries great attraction, a period that signaled a historic turning point in fashion history, with the spread of patterns and styles that have since then influenced the feminine look for a great deal of time.

These patterns were **practical and feminine at the same time**, and they reflected the **changes that were taking place in society and also within families**.

The style in vogue in that period, although subsequently overtaken by the following trends, continued to maintain **indisputable appeal** for decades. And today it's been reaffirming itself once again by reinventing styles and outfits that, although yanked from the past, seem more current than ever.

The unquestionable success of this style can be chalked up to numerous determining factors that have been acting in harmony. Among these there are two principally fundamental ones: the invention of **ready-to-wear** items on the one hand and rising **feminine independence** on the other.

The diffusion of ready-to-wear resulted in an upheaval to the traditional conception of attire based on tailor-made clothes, which were put together and tailored according to the physique of each single client. **Ready-to-wear made fashionable clothes much more accessible to all women**, thanks to lower prices and the possibility of finding, even in the biggest stores, items of good quality. Secondly, the patterns had to adjust to a new reality that witnessed **women becoming so much more emancipated and independent** than they'd been in the past. The corset fell into disuse. Rigid and uncomfortable cuts were abandoned, totally ill-suited to everyday tasks. Knit garments exploded all over. The increasing use of the washing machine demanded less delicate textiles. Patterns, while remaining feminine, became more fluid than in the past.

All of this led to what we could define as a genuinely real **small revolution of fashion**, but this revolution didn't come about by erasing all that had occurred previously; quite the opposite, **it maintained a strong connection to the past**, guaranteeing it a long-enduring success.

In fact, it was precisely *because* ready-to-wear was just starting out that the patterns, styles, and colors, while being more practical and easily wearable, drew inspiration from the patterns of the previous era, when tailors and seamstresses sewed clothes according to an individual's measurements.

The standardized patterns and cuts with little differentiation from one to the other had yet to become widespread and were only introduced in the decades to come at the expense of quality and wearability.

Similarly, **textiles at this time were still high-quality fabrics made to stand the test of time**, even if they were simpler than the ones used for high fashion. This also allowed them to be washed in the first washing machines that had just appeared on the market.

With the arrival of ready-to-wear items, patterns became more practical while maintaining their feminine characteristics of elegance from another era

To reflect this **new image of the woman, feminine and determined at the same time**, clothing was **practical but elegant**, traditionalist but innovative, and **seductive but refined**. This ensured an extremely well taken care of look that was always practical and successful.

Subsequently, **since the '60s**, women have predominantly been dressing in ways that symbolized instead a radical **desire for change** with respect to the past.

Clothing had become a way to express dissatisfaction with the old traditionalist guard of the fashion world, completely subverting all the patterns in vogue until that moment from an aesthetic point of view—but not exclusively.

These stylistic models were **unisex in form, with mostly oversized garments that didn't comply with one's shape**, and those items became almost exclusively the uniform of youth.

The high-quality and well-made textiles of old were replaced by lower-quality fabrics, making it that much more difficult to get a well-crafted look, something that in any case was looked down upon as unfashionable.

This new model, although dulled by the reappearance somewhere around the 1980s of clothes with a more traditionalist stamp, signified the almost total disappearance of those quality-driven traits that characterized fashion in previous eras. This didn't apply only to fabrics and patterns but also to wider aspects like color, for example. So much so that even today, if a color isn't considered hot, it's practically impossible to find clothes with that tint (and we're not even talking about sea foam green or baby blue...even simple yellows, reds, or blues). On the contrary, **black**, a color that in the past was largely worn by the less wealthy, has become completely **ubiquitous among the fashionable**, whereas in the past the upper classes generally selected clothing with wonderful colors and prints.

Fortunately, as I've been saying since the beginning of this chapter, an authentically modern twist involving the **rediscovery of styles and patterns from the past** has been occurring now for quite some time.

The woman defined today as **curvy**, for example, has **resurfaced as a benchmark pattern of reference**, exactly as she was in the past.

Patterns and cuts made for non-normative shapes or decidedly nonstatuesque figures are all over the place these days, and this allows each one of us to set the tone for a style that seamlessly conforms to our physique and to our personality.

If we want to have an awesome and breathtaking look, then rediscovering and **refashioning styles and trends taken from the past according to current tastes, needs, and habits** can be useful and fun.

This by no means implies having a classic look or something so traditionalist it hurts to look at. It simply means **repositioning what was once better some time ago and reusing it to our advantage**, something we can adapt over time to both our personal style but also to specific occasions.

The most important places we can find inspiration in the past can be divided into three categories: **fabrics, patterns, and colors**.

TEXTILES

One of the most essential things to rediscover—which among other things nowadays is quite in vogue—is making sure we're using **high-quality fabrics**, or fabrics of a particular make, like much of what we saw in the second part of the book.

The material an item of clothing is made from is without a doubt one of the most important elements of a garment. It allows us to always have a well-cared-for image and to appear at our tiptop best, **enhancing our physique and making our wardrobe management that much easier** and faster.

To give you an example, not so long ago I was in a shop and I happened to find a sweater that was almost identical to one that I've had and worn for years thanks to its exceptional quality, one of those items you can wear in all occasions and feel totally put together. Obviously, I was so satisfied with the find that I snatched it up right away, without bothering to stop and check out the material, but the result, in the end, was incredibly disappointing. After washing it, the new sweater lost all its form, and when I wore it the sweater came off as ragged and saggy, suitable at best as a beach robe, gifting me with a few extra pounds around the waist and a smaller breast size, which was a pretty disappointing outcome, considering that I'm already an A-cup. The difference between the two pieces of clothing was, obviously, uniquely found in the fabric, confirming once more the importance of the quality of the textile so much more than the brand, the pattern, and even the color. The same color that can brighten up our faces if the fabric is beautifully luminous can, at the same time, make us seem tired if it's low quality. Give it a try and have your mind blown by the result.

Vintage fabrics can be reinterpreted for contemporary times guaranteeing a sophisticated result thanks to the quality of the material

The advice, then, is to **refine your knowledge of fabrics and yarns**, a knowledge that our grandmothers possessed almost instinctually and which in recent times has all but disappeared, in part thanks to the diffusion of industrial fabrics of miserable quality. Doing this, we'll be able to have a bit of fun **enriching our**

look by playing with different textures and materials, guaranteeing us an appearance that's always impeccable and form-fitted for all occasions, even if we're wearing practical and simple items.

PATTERNS

Reusing patterns recovered from the past gives you the enormous advantage of **choosing from a practically unlimited range of garments to find the item that's most suited to your physique**.

At this moment, this is seen especially in makers of jeans, who are putting out in large-scale—from the most expensive brands to the cheapest—all their principal patterns: from tight skinny jeans to the classic cigarette jeans and from the bootcut style to the more ample boyfriend jeans, high-waist and low-waist styles, and so on.

In reality, even for other pieces of clothing, we can find, with just a bit of patience, nearly personalized patterns or, at least, options that can be personalized for every physique under the sun.

Patterns of such variety allow those of us carrying a few extra pounds to wear **feminine and elegant clothes, getting rid of all those formless items called plus-sized that do nothing but devalue womanly curves by hiding the most feminine points** of each woman.

So we can relish in the excitement of discovering our style by choosing from many different patterns inspired by the best aspects of every era.

From empire-style dresses to those cinched at the waist, from pleated skirts to flared ones, from cloth cloaks to the classic gabardine trench coat, we can let ourselves go wild finding inspiration in each style and period that we love, **always finding something that speaks to us and has us feeling our best** no matter what, recovering it from the past but with an eye toward the future.

PARTE THREE: TIMELESS CHARME

A timeless classic: a knee-length overcoat worn with a straight-line dress gives us a foolproof outfit, always chic and form-fitted for various occasions

COLORS

Even with colors, it can be useful and interesting to get inspiration from the innumerable shades that were once found in the past.

A primary starting point for reflection comes from the observation that **the omnipresent shade of black**—officially legitimized by Coco Chanel, considered perfect for every occasion, and widely used by all of us because it looks good on everyone and slims the figure—***doesn't*, in reality, look good on everyone**.

Remember that there was once a time when women wore black only when they were forced to; the famous writer Agatha

Christie, talking about the economic hardships at the beginning of her married life, remembered it well, as she had just "one evening dress, and that would be a black one so as not to show the dirt, and when we went out on muddy evenings, I would always, of course, have black shoes for the same reason."

The widespread use of black, moreover, has also brought about some occasionally unsatisfying results, because there's also a disadvantage to this color, as mentioned earlier: it can **harden the features and make wrinkles more visible**, especially for those with dark hair.

If we really want to wear black, we may want to **take advantage of some tricks that soften the effects it has on the face**, like a low collar, for example, rather than a high one, or a scarf or a necklace, highly useful for softening the features, especially for those with brown or black hair.

If it's a personalized look that we're after, then we can also try to switch up black with other colors; if it's true that dark tones slim, then it's equally true that **there is an inordinate amount of dark colors that we can make use of with the same slimming effect** of black.

So another simple tip, if we're still trying to get the slimming effect, is choosing darker colors for skirts or pants and a similar color that's just slightly lighter for the top. Paired with a light-colored necklace, bone, for example, or colored stones or some shiny element, this would be perfect.

Besides, remember that if it's true that black colors trim our figures, then even the lighter shades, as we've pointed out before, can have the same effect if used from top to bottom.

Of course, during winter it's neither easy nor feasible to dress all in white or in beige, but in spring and summer not only is it easily doable, but it's even a light and practical way to dress. In particular **at the beginning of the summer**, when we haven't been too sun-kissed yet, **a light-colored dress can trim much more than an identical dress in a dark color** that contrasts with our not-so-tanned legs by highlighting the most robust parts of our figure.

PARTE THREE: TIMELESS CHARME

*Light-colored garments, worn without tights or with transparent tights,
can have the same slimming effect of dark colors
as long as they're in tone with the legs and the arms*

Getting back to the theme of color selection, one element that most definitely hinders our choices is the fact that **it's not always easy to find the shades or tones we're looking for** in the stores. The colors of the garments are generally always the same save for a few tints in vogue for the current season.

How can we get ourselves a more personalized, greater range of choices? Once again in this case, we can find interesting alternatives waiting for us in the past.

One solution that might seem challenging at first but in reality is easier than it sounds is to make, on our own, some articles of clothing, freely choosing fabrics and yarns and drawing inspiration from magazines and specialized publications. Or we could make some strategic changes to garments that we already own, transforming them into something completely different in a few minutes just with the addition of some details (edges, cuffs, or collars, for example), using different colors or materials.

Another opportunity, as simple as it is uncommon, is to **dye the clothes**. Fabric dye can be easily found in every supermarket, big box store, or on-line and can be used in washing machines with absolute simplicity (and free of any damages, guaranteed). We can use dyes to either **renew items with faded color or change an existing tone** of a color that we never really liked, making these garments seem like new again because they can attain a new life, ushering in a breath of innovation into our wardrobe.

Besides, every dye produces a different color according to many different factors, like the tone of the original color and the composition and quality of the textile: the more beautiful the textile, the better the effect of the new color will be. But it also depends on the quantity of clothing you put into dye (the less clothing you toss in the washing machine, the more intense the newly obtained color will be, while the more you throw in, the lighter the color). **By using fabric dye and minimal effort, you can get like-new clothes with eye-catching colors without having to resort to custom-made.**

Consider giving it a try: you'll see that you can create truly unusual colors that every friend of yours will want to copy.

These few simple steps are more than sufficient to produce an absolutely captivating effect for an outfit in which **every item will seem to complete the others naturally** without giving off an artificial or overly elaborate vibe.

You'll find yourself with **a pleasantly retro look**, which by contrast will have you appearing fresher and more harmonious, befitting of any woman with *charme*.

XXI. Timeless Style: The Appeal of Personality

> *Nature gives you the face you have at twenty; it's up to you to merit the face you have at fifty.*
> —Coco Chanel

On my mother's side of the family, there are five sisters (my mother and my aunts) with an average age of seventy. There's also another aunt who's into her eighties, plus their various cousins, all in their seventies.

All these women, despite their age, are *beautiful* women, and each one is attractive in her own unique way, not only because of their different features (some are taller and some are shorter, some are quite thin and some are shapelier, some have a round face and some have a more angular face) but more than anything because of their different personalities and so, consequently, also because of their styles.

There's the artist aunt; there's the irreducibly green one. There's the one always focusing on the trends and another classically fashionable, and another still who, after having done the trendy look in her youth, has come to prefer a sportier and more informal look but is no less fascinating because of it.

Some were beautiful even from a young age, while others didn't feel all that striking in their twenties and thirties. They **found their *charme* and beauty only in the passing of years and with a greater degree of self-understanding**.

There's one common denominator that unites all these women: they understand themselves and they celebrate themselves for what and who they are, highlighting and emphasizing each one of their distinct personalities thanks to their **positive and vital character**.

Even when confronting life's difficulties, they've always handled things and themselves positively and energetically, using these difficulties like an instrument to help their own strength and determination grow instead of seeing them as obstacles.

This confirms once more the single true secret of *charme* and allure: our personality, from which and not by chance our style arrives.

Those who are able to find the necessary will and determination to overcome all of life's difficulties, both big and small, can call upon an indefatigable source of energy inside themselves that shows on their face and in their way of interacting with others.

Those who possess this calm reserve are made irresistible and enchanting. As Coco Chanel once said, "You can be gorgeous at thirty, charming at forty, and irresistible for the rest of your life."

For this reason, one of the essential elements when it comes to maintaining allure and vitality even as the years pass is **the desire to cultivate our own personality and accept ourselves for what we are**. At the same time, however, we must try to smooth out our little imperfections and play directly to our strengths.

Now that's a rule that applies as much to our personality as it does to our physique: those who can manage to get the first thing down can easily go on to manage the second almost as though it were automatic and spontaneous.

Each one of us, after all, despite the influence of fashion, wants one thing more than anything else: **to be different from the rest**. Through a prudent and critical analysis of our personality and ourselves, that's a goal we can reach with certainty and ease.

All the types of styles we've seen so far, not surprisingly, correspond to the different shades of personality. Despite being different from each other, they are all characterized by some particularities held in common. For example, they have a **strong identity**. They're invulnerable to the passage of time and the shifting of the trends, in the sense that **they maintain a formidable allure even amid the changing trends** because they have a sense of harmony and equilibrium impermeable to time's march. Beyond that, they are all characterized by a strong sense of self-criticism, which allows them to see themselves as they truly are, not as they wish they were.

Two contrasting looks that are equal in their charme: the harmony of patterns and colors brings out the best in every figure and never goes out of style

Not to be overlooked is the fact that **our imperfections** (real or imagined) **can even have a positive outcome on our image**. Paradoxically, what we deem to be our weak points are truly the aspects of ourselves that gift us the possibility to be more enchanting and put together—just as much as if not more so than those who, in our eyes, don't have any imperfections at all.

Those who think they're imperfect, interestingly enough, often redirect this perception into a deeper form of taking care of themselves in an attentive search for what brings out our best qualities, which gives us the possibility of reaching our maximum potential.

Meanwhile, those who seemingly begin with more gifts endowed by nature often pay the price for it with the passing of the years, mostly because the habit of not having to take great care of yourself can take hold with time, becoming difficult to adjust down the road.

Beyond this, it's fundamental not to limit ourselves to aesthetic canons imposed from year to year according to momentary trends, which often fail to play to the strengths of our physique and our way of being feminine.

Another thing that's essential is masterfully **taking advantage of the practically infinite range of styles and shades** with which we can let our femininity fly, succeeding in creating an image of ourselves that satisfies us and reflects us in the fullest way possible.

On the other hand, it's equally true that we women generally have a mutable and complex personality that sometimes even appears completely different depending on our state of mind or mood or on the people around us.

So how do we reconcile this with our style choices?

Simple—by indulging in and sublimating the sensations of the moment. What I mean by this is **allowing us some inroads in different styles when we feel them close to us**, even if only for a little while, maybe even for just a night.

But be aware that in order to get the best results, this choice should always be *conscious*. The style we choose doesn't necessarily have to remain the same, but once we find exactly what it is that suits us the most and fits our personalities, we can reinterpret it in a different way every time in a kind of dialogue with other styles.

Not only is our predominant character represented by succeeding in this way, but also our most intimate and hidden sides, which beyond helping us feel good about ourselves can help us feel at ease even with those around us.

This way, our choices will allow us to arrive at an overall unique solution that can truly be immensely satisfying, not to mention **irresistibly stylish and incredibly charming at any age**.

XXII. Wrapping It All Up in Beauty: The 7 Rules of Style (And Some Clichés to Demystify)

Fashion is what gets recommended but which is often best to avoid. Style is what each one of us has and which must be conserved for a lifetime.
—Giorgio Armani

To conclude, let's look together at some basic guidelines that briefly summarize the main topics discussed in this book, to know **how to make the right style choices**, and obtain a result that satisfies us in every way possible. It's important to avoid fashion stereotypes: in terms of style, pursuing commonplace ideas can often be counterproductive. Conversely, choosing a personal, unique style that works great on you is definitely the winning choice.

Charme and Style Require a Bloated Budget:
FALSE

Though it may sound unbelievable to many, this really is just a myth. Instead, **the very fact of wanting to respect our budget often allows us to find ingenious, out-of-the-ordinary solutions that make our unique**.

Remember that the one thing that's fundamental for achieving a unique allure is a harmony of the colors and forms with a respect for proportions, none of which has anything to do with our budget.

If we choose an outfit in which the items work together in a delicate harmony—or even in *wild* harmony, according to our personality—then our outfit will have far more style than a look composed of items thrown together to show off the label as the only criterion rather than good taste.

We should never forget the words of Ralph Lauren: "Fashion is not necessarily about labels. It's not about brands. It's about something else that comes from within you."

And if you really are dying to have an expensive garment, then before anything **bet on quality and not a brand or a trend**, and then keep in mind that it's combining fine articles of clothing with other more simply made ones that brings about the best results.

Broadly speaking, for garments such as outerwear, shoes, and bags, it's better if they're well made (which *doesn't* necessarily mean branded or expensive!), while blouses, tops, scarves, jeans, and skirts can offer more than satisfying solutions even if you find them at a low price. This guarantees you'll be able to reach a good compromise between aesthetics and cost, because **the valuable clothes create a kind of "pulling" effect on the others**, giving off the idea of an outfit composed of only exclusive items.

I Have to Have a Ton of Clothes and Accessories to Be Sure I Can Always Find the Right Combinations: *FALSE*

As we've seen at length in previous chapters, what counts most when it comes to attaining a stylish image is fundamentally the *quality* of the garments rather than their *quantity* in our closets. Quality not quantity is always better—fewer items but those made with knowing hands rather than a slew of items made poorly that don't bring us any satisfaction. As Giorgio Armani once stated: "The difference between style and fashion is quality." When we say *quality,* we mean three things: **a lovely fabric, a good cut, and a fine manufacture of the item.**

And don't forget that the only yardstick in this field is our own eyes, not the number of garments we have stuffed in our closets!

When checking ourselves out in front of the mirror, if we have **a sensation of harmony and pleasure**, then we're on the right track, and we can more easily reach this result by *removing* some items rather than adding. As Coco Chanel famously advised: "Before you leave the house, look in the mirror and remove one accessory."

The items we choose for our wardrobe—whether they be office clothes or the garments reserved for galas and nights out—don't necessarily need to be superabundant, but they *do* have to give the idea of complementing one another, of **blending together into a unique and irreproducible outfit**.

If instead our appearance gives off the sensation of being overloaded—even if every single item is beautiful and expensive—then this indicates that something has to change and we need to reconsider our outfit.

If I Want to Be Considered *Fashionable*, I Must Buy a Lot of Items of the Most Current Trends Every Single Year: *FALSE*

The basic rules of feminine allure are essentially the same, and they're based on the idea of **focusing all our attention on the outfit in its entirety** rather than on any other single element.

The first task to take on, as we have seen in the previous pages, is deciding which style sings to us most loudly and clearly. But what does that even mean? Well, though this may sound obvious and repetitive, it means directing our attention not so much toward single items and accessories—skirts, necklaces, belts—but rather toward the *whole* outfit, which must above all else align with our personality, our lifestyle, our habits, and our passions. All of which is to say that it must be rooted in **something that doesn't waver with the passing of a few months**, unlike trends and fashions.

Once we've solidified the style that screams our name at full volume, the selection of single items or garments is all but automatic. And by doing this, we allow ourselves to **pick out our personal "evergreen" items and combinations that never lose their luster**, continuing to bring us joy throughout the years. These can be adapted here or there to different times and various occasions, all thanks to small and very simple adjustments.

And of course, no matter our age or the place, our appearance will always be eye-catching and alluring.

The use of timeless clothing items brings out an absolutely trendy look but one that's impervious to the instability of trends

If I Don't Follow What's in Fashion, I Will Have an Unkempt Look and Won't Be "In":
FALSE

As we have seen in other chapters, we can look absolutely in style—if that's what we want—even *without* following the trends (where *trends* describes in-vogue garments that will soon be irretrievably branded as outdated if not even in bad taste).

It seems like a paradox, but this is the way it is. The secret comes down to two essential points: choosing between what is in vogue at the moment and what best suits your body. Make your style yours and **find, in contemporary trends, those that can be considered "classics"** (there are always some: you just have to pay attention to them).

Let me share a practical example: if yellow ochre, military green, and navy blue are all the rage this year, and you are a blonde with some lighter highlights, the first two colors will look terrible on you, but navy blue will look just perfect. Moreover, navy blue is an *evergreen* choice (which means that you can always wear items of this color even if it's not the current trend).

For this reason, you should take out all your blue clothing to wear, of course adding something new if you want. You can thereby create your own complete look in and of itself that is incredibly in vogue, uniquely your own, and you won't find yourself getting rid of your clothing items the following year!

Similarly, if one year the most in-vogue items are multicolored bags, ruffled shirts, and cigarette pants, you can let go of the first two and splurge on the latest, which you can use in coming years without being out-of-date.

There Are Rules That Are Suitable for Everyone of All Ages That Always Make You Feel Marvelous:
TRUE

There are a few simple rules that we have encountered in previous chapters. Out of all of them, the most important one to follow to make sure you have a unique appeal is also the most difficult: **simplicity**. Coco Chanel summed up this desirable aspiration in her famous quote, "Simplicity is the keynote of all true elegance." **The fewer garments you have on, the cleaner, more fascinating, and more recognizable your style will be**.

What does this mean?

It means, for example, that if you wear a much sought-after garment or a very eccentric bag, then neither necklaces, bracelets, nor belts should be overly showy. Some will rightly object: "OK, but how do I keep my pants on without a belt?" Easy: simply choose a "nonbelt," a smooth belt that is in the same tone as your trousers or accessories. And that's it.

Geometric cuts and foolproof outfits allow fresh and sober-minded ensembles that are undeniably classy

There Are Trends That We Could Define as Evergreen, Which Means Always in Fashion:
TRUE

For instance, the current trends use a lot of neutral colors that are rediscovered in all their nuances not only for clothes but in accessories such as handbags and shoes: despite having been proposed recently, these styles have always existed, albeit in a minor way. **Due to this timelessness, these fashions can therefore be defined as a true evergreen**.

Generally, tone-on-tone or more shades of the same color compliment both curvier and thinner figures and enhance the overall look. If you feel too thin, a little plump, or a little short, the use of graduated colors will balance your figure and make you look more harmonious and proportionate. The addition of one to two brightly colored accessories will add character to your outfit without detracting from the whole ensemble.

Among other things, balancing the figure as a whole can also be achieved with magnificent results by using intense tones that result in a charming effect.

As for lines and shapes, there is great interest in the reuse of vintage patterns that are remade in newer materials or outfit combinations that differ from traditional ones.

Combining new garments with vintage ones allows us to enrich our look in a timeless way. An interesting and fun idea is to take a vintage item and turn it by ourselves into something new. I often do it myself: it is fun to play with a needle and thread and figure out the best place to add a few darts or tweak the line of a dress to get a completely different and exciting fit.

I Can Always Find Trends That Complement My Physique:
TRUE

With increased attention to everything that is connected to personal well-being on both a physical and mental level, this harmony will also be visually reflected in what we wear.

In my opinion, the future will bring an increasing emergence of new ensembles that **combine beauty with practicality** that will give off pleasant sensations from a visual, physical, and tactile point of perspective.

PARTE THREE: TIMELESS CHARME

An optical trick to slim the figure: a partly opened coat worn over contrasting colors trims the silhouette, making it look slimmer

The consistency of the fabrics, their texture, and the feel of the material that the garment is made from—for example, raw linen, wool, and certain types of stitching—can be important playful elements that give personality to our look.

These formal aspects of clothing make us more pleasing first of all to ourselves, and then to those around us.

Another positive trend is the evolution of very intense colors that until recently had only appeared as accents alongside bright colors, and then evolved to an increasing use of captivating but "neutral" shades. This way you wind up with **splendid versatile tones, true color classics** that combine easily to create timeless looks and that can be chosen in shades that best suit us to help illuminate the face and soften our features.

The growing choices when it comes to cuts, colors, and fabrics allows us to identify trends that fit our taste, physique, and personality, whatever the momentary fads are.

It's important only to know how to select what works best for you, but if you have read this book, you now know it. That said, the job is done.

You have customized your choices.

And your choices will always be in style.

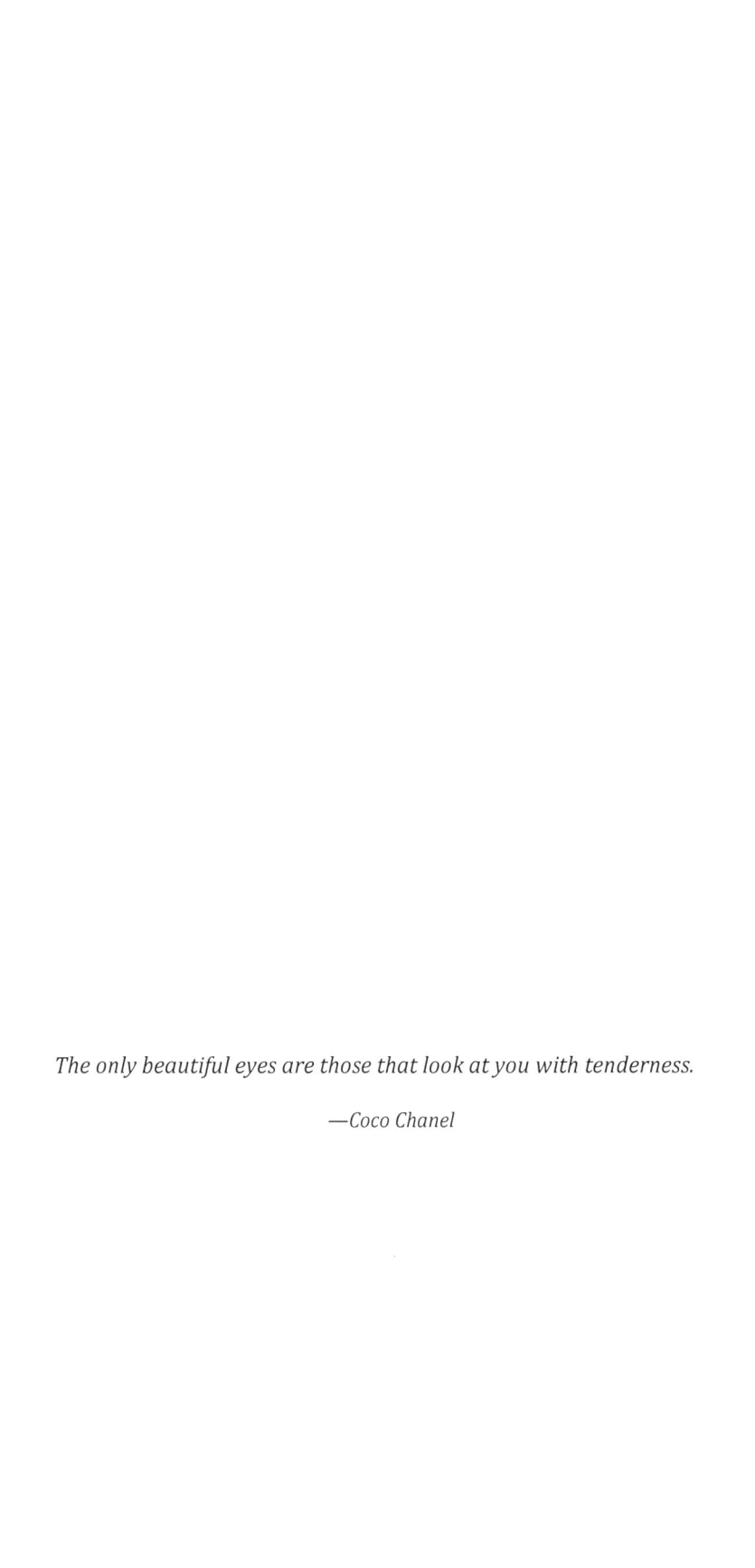

The only beautiful eyes are those that look at you with tenderness.

—*Coco Chanel*

APPENDIX

FABRICS AND TEXTILES
The Weave of Style

TEXTILES

COTTON

Cotton is obtained through the processing of yarn obtained from the hair that covers the seeds of a plant, thus making it a plant-based material characterized by the lightness and freshness of its touch. Although it is currently highly popular, its diffusion is relatively recent, since the Arabs introduced it in Europe only around the fourteenth century. Until then, in Europe fabrics were made mainly in linen, hemp, and wool. Cotton can be used to produce several different kinds of fabric, including jersey, which combines the comfort of cotton fabric with the elasticity of knit textiles.

WOOL

Wool is obtained from the shearing of the hair of sheep and other animals, including rabbits, camels, llamas, and goats. The famous cashmere wool, for example, is produced from the wool of a goat that lives in the Asian highlands. The animal's fiber is characterized by the presence of elastic corrugations that give the wool elasticity, softness, and high thermal insulation capacities, making it warm to the touch. For the same reason, wool can protect not only against the cold but also the heat. Because of its poor mechanical strength and resistance to high temperature, it cannot be used in technical and industrial fabrics. Nonetheless, it is widely used in handicraft sectors thanks to its high quality and assorted varieties and features, allowing it to be used to produce many products.

LINEN

Linen is obtained by maceration of the stem of herbaceous plants. It is undoubtedly one of the oldest textiles, as it was known and already used in the fifth millennium BC. The Babylonians, the Phoenicians, the Egyptians (the production and processing of linen are also documented in the Egyptian tombs and in the pyramids) and other peoples of the Middle East all cultivated it. Linen reached its peak in Europe in the Middle Ages, and for centuries it was one of the most widely used textiles until the nineteenth century when, thanks to the Industrial Revolution, cotton-spinning machines gave rise to the prevalence of cotton. Since then, the spread of linen has decreased rapidly, but thanks to its freshness and softness—whether used alone or in combination with other fibers helping to improve its mechanical performance—it's still a product appreciated by many.

HEMP

The use of hemp for producing fabrics was very common in ancient times, especially in Asia and Europe, where it had been cultivated since the third millennium AD. Thanks to its extremely strong fibers, for centuries it was used extensively in producing clothing of any kind (in particular for those of daily use). A vegetable-based fiber much like cotton and linen, it was one of the most-used raw materials for fabric production until the last century. However, clothes made with hemp had the disadvantage of being fairly rough and stiff, and for these reasons cotton eventually replaced it almost completely. Today, thanks to new production methods that have made hemp fabrics soft and more comfortable, hemp fibers have recently seen a resurgence in the textile industry.

SILK

Silk is produced though the transformation of a filament that comes from the shelter produced by silkworms. Using this method, it is possible to produce precious fabrics that are highly distinguished for their softness and brightness. Historically, the use of silk originated in China, probably around 3000 BC. Initially the practice of sericulture was kept secret at the orders of the Chinese emperors. However, farmers later began to move to other areas, eventually arriving in Italy and from there to the rest of Europe (around AD 500). In Italy, the breeding of silkworms and the production and trade of silk were a very profitable industry for a long time (in Florence, the *Arte della Seta*, or "silk art," was recognized as one of the seven Major Guilds), but in recent times it has totally disappeared due not only to changes in agricultural organization, but also due to the low prices of synthetic fibers.

However, its softness, brightness, and pleasant touch are unmatched, allowing silk to remain an extraordinary product, resisting, especially in the long term, any and all competition from synthetic fabrics. In industrial production, it is sometimes combined with wool or other fibers to increase its elasticity and thus its range of possibility.

VISCOSE AND OTHER ARTIFICIAL FIBERS

Artificial fibers, along with the synthetic ones that we will see in the next section, do not exist in nature, but are the result of an industrial process. They were produced first in the late nineteenth century and were developed further with industrialization.

Mainly made of cellulose, they differ depending on the type of process used to produce them: the main and most frequently used artificial fabrics are viscose or rayon (also called artificial silk), together with acetate, cupro, and modal.

These fibers are often combined with natural fibers to improve the mechanical characteristics of natural materials. Since they're vegetable-based (although resulting from further industrial processing), they can guarantee a better breathability than some wholly synthetic fibers.

SYNTHETIC FIBERS

Invented in the 1930s and 1940s (and thus more recently than artificial fibers), synthetic fibers are produced by molecules obtained via synthesis. More precisely, they are derived from the processing of very cheap petroleum-derived raw materials, transformed with chemical reactions. The most used fibers for clothing are polyester, acrylic, polyamide (nylon), spandex (polyurethane), and Gore-Tex. Compared to other materials of natural origin, they can be produced in a virtually infinite range of variations and possess the advantage of not losing color and ensuring a high breathability and an exceptional insulating power, especially newer materials. However, they do have some drawbacks. Synthetic fibers are generally not biodegradable and they harbor a greater allergenic risk.

MANUFACTURING

CANVAS

Canvas is the most common type of fabric, obtained from the interweaving of a weft and a warp, which are merely intertwined without the presence of other processes. Despite the fairly simple production process involved in creating canvas, it is possible to obtain beautiful fabrics that are all different from each other depending on the thickness of the threads and their color. Many types of fabric are in fact simply canvases that differ in the raw materials used or according to the different finishes and machining processes.

For example, beginning with the weaving itself, dyed canvas yarn differs in use from different color threads, which result in very exquisite-looking fabrics. By contrast, if the design on a fabric is obtained as a result of printing on a white canvas, the final effect is less sophisticated.

WOOL FELT

Wool felt is obtained from wool by "felting" it to make it waterproof. Felting is the name of the process that closes the interstices between the threads and brushes it on one side to obtain the characteristic "hairy" look.

It is a very heavy fabric with a high resistance to wear and tear, as long as its waterproof and windproof aspects are working right, while at the same time remaining breathable. Thanks to these features, it has been used for a long time in the creation of jackets and coats. With the discovery of synthetic fibers and waterproofing materials, its use has decreased, but some designers have recently rediscovered it and used it in their new collections, giving new life to a product that, although of ancient origin, has properties and characteristics that make it extremely versatile.

VOILE and ORGANDY

Voile is a type of canvas made with very thin threads that are then used to produce a nearly transparent fabric, soft and light but at the same time resistant.

It can be made from silk, cotton, or synthetic materials, and it is typically used for scarves, undergarments, nightgowns, and blouses. If they are properly lined to reduce transparency, dresses can even be made of voile.

Organdy, which is also obtained from thinly threaded canvas of cotton, silk, or synthetic fibers, is similar to voile in terms of lightness and transparency but much more rigid.

When different colors are used for the weft and the warp, the result is the characteristic iridescent effect (also obtainable for other types of fabric), which is mainly used for formal wear or accessories.

DENIM and MOLESKIN

Denim, the fabric largely used in the manufacture of classic jeans, is in a certain way the evolution of the oldest moleskin, which we could easily get away with considering as its ancestor. The main difference between the two shows up in the color of the warp and weft: in moleskin, warp and weft are the same color, while in denim the weave is usually white (or another light color), and the web is typically blue. The special finish that gives to moleskin a look that seems almost velvety is another difference between moleskin and denim.

Both are obtained with a type of weaving called *twill* (which is different from canvas) that is characterized by a propensity for diagonals and by presenting a front side and a back side that are different from each other, adding softness and resistance to the fabric. Thanks to these features, what we end up with are fabrics that can be used for work wear as well as for more casual, everyday purposes.

GABARDINE

Gabardine is similar to denim in that they both derive from a weave characterized by a manufacturing process that favors a diagonal pattern.

It differs from denim with its sleek finish, characterized by an inclined and compact rib stitch that's more visible on the front side than the backside, and it can be made of cotton, wool, or artificial fiber.

It is a smart-looking fabric that can still feel comfortable despite its heaviness. Thanks to its characteristics, it is often used in jackets and raincoats, the classic trench coat being the first among them.

TWEED and TARTAN

Like the previous fabrics, tweed is a type of wool with diagonal weaving. The texture in this case can be both simple and combinable with any number of others: for example, the classic herringbone fabric, made up by opposite-sitting diagonal tilt stitches with alternating light and dark colors that represent the most conventional and classic type of tweed.

It is a soft fabric that is at the same time very durable and high quality, and it is typically used to produce coats, jackets, pants, and suits.

It can also be realized with the classic colors of tartan, a term that indicates the particular fabric designs produced in the Scottish Highlands, obtained with threads of different colors that correspond to the colors of the ancient local clans.

Though it is basically a classic fabric, recently it has been reinterpreted to create extremely trendy clothes (but also accessories), suitable even for younger women.

VELVET

Velvet is a type of fabric that can be defined as *double-cloth,* which means that it consists of multiple warps and wefts. Velvet has two warps and one weft.

Mainly made in cotton, it may also be obtained from wool or silk, although velvets obtained from such raw material are less used.

Velvet is characterized by it's "hairy" appearance on one side (a trait suggestive of the word's origins, *vellus* meaning "hair" in Latin), and can be worked in different ways, with corduroy, ribbed, and embossed (exposed to pressure to obtain on the fabric's surface the permanent imprint of a given design) being some of the most well-known. For centuries in Europe, velvet was used exclusively by the aristocracy and the wealthy classes, thanks to its sophisticated and refined appearance and its soothing touch, which made it extremely pleasant and one of the more well-loved fabrics.

Recently, it has been rediscovered by some designers, who have brought it back to popularity not only for jackets, coats, and suits, but also for accessories like handbags and shoes.

PIQUÉ

Piqué (the term comes from the French word meaning "to pinch, to poke") is a double-cloth fabric that consists of two warps and two wefts. It is characterized by small motifs in relief (dots, diamonds, squares) that give a kind of quilted effect that ends up feeling very soft to the touch and comfortable to wear.

It is made generally in cotton, sometimes combined with mixed fibers for a better fit.

As a fresh and light fabric, it is particularly suited to the warm months: not surprisingly, the classic polo shirt is made from this fabric.

SATIN

Satin has a very uniform appearance, thanks to the fact that the fastenings between warp and weft are very sparse.

This type of fabric, traditionally made of silk but more recently produced from cotton or via synthetic fibers, has a shiny appearance on one side where the warp is most prevalent and a matte appearance on the other side, where the weft is more evident.

Its development is closely linked to the history of silk, with which it was produced for centuries, and so it was always considered a refined and sophisticated fabric thanks in particular to its characteristic luster.

Since this is a particularly delicate fabric, it is suitable for items like ties, shirts, or decorative elements (ribbons), but also elegant women's garments.

KNITWEAR

Knitwear is formed by a weft of threads that are free of warp and weft and realized via the use of needles, crochet, or knitting machines. The history of industrial knitting is interesting. The first machine that produced this kind of fabric was designed in the late sixteenth century by the Englishman William Lee, who then had to emigrate to France because his invention was banned by the British Crown, which feared competition for English women who were producing knitted garments by hand. Subsequently, the industrial revolution caused the necessary mechanization also of knitting machines, further increasing the diffusion of this type of fabric. Coco Chanel provided an additional boost to its spread when she introduced knitted fabrics to her collections, thus giving way to the realization of items that combined elegance with practicality. This fabric can be processed in a simple or complex way, giving rise to different-looking fabrics, smooth, ribbed, or with many other patterns. It is characterized by a high elasticity that can be higher or lower depending on the type of machining, and it can be obtained from any textile fiber, although the most used are wool, cotton, and viscose.

Jersey is a shaved-looking type of mesh comprising the majority of all industrially produced knitwear, and it's a fabric that should be used with great caution unless it's opportunely reinforced and supported, because it tends to highlight the critical aspects of one's figure.

LACE

Lace is a special processing of the yarn that allows you to get a fabric with a really delicate appearance. For centuries, it was produced exclusively by hand, and for this reason it was considered extremely valuable in consideration of the time necessary to obtain even a small piece of cloth.

In recent times, thanks to the introduction of machineries, lace has experienced an increasing popularity thanks to the lowering of its price. However, the uniqueness of hand-made lace remains unchanged, arising from the fact that these fabrics are virtually unique products made with maximum craftsmanship. They have become highly sought after items in all the vintage shops. The most widespread of manufacturing processes is the soft and elegant Chantilly lace, the Sangallo lace, and macramé, which instead is kind of a heavy and consistent lace made with a knotted weave so that it can easily take on large designs.

ABOUT THE AUTHOR

Chiara Giuliani, an architect with a passion for style and fashion, lives in Florence, Italy. After some academic and professional publications, in 2012 she published her first book, La Casa di Charme, *a manual for making your home your own unique place, showing how to identify what is most in tune with your own character and how to create a warm and cozy environment at once easy to live in and simple to maintain.*
In 2016, she published her second book, La Donna di Charme, *a manual of personal style to provide women of all ages and types with the tools to build their self-confidence by enhancing their strong points and help them feel more beautiful and attractive everywhere and in every way.*

Her motto comes from a famous quote:

**Beauty begins
the moment you decide
to be yourself**.
—Coco Chanel

Follow us on Instagram
@ladonnadicharme

info@ladonnadicharme.it
www.ladonnadicharme.it

Printed in Poland
by Amazon Fulfillment
Poland Sp. z o.o., Wrocław